The Great UN-Reset

Humanity's Battle Against a Dystopian New World Order

Constantine du Bruyn

Castle Vale Publishers Ltd. London

This book is dedicated to all the 'conspiracy theorists' out there, who were just too early with the truth.

It's for those who are willing to open their minds to the contents of this book.

It's for my precious children and all the other children of our future.

Finally and lovingly, this is for my wife, to thank her for allowing me the freedom to explore 'the crazy', as she *used* to call it.

Contents

Introduction

The world is a very strange place, and it is often difficult to discern the truth from fiction. In the quest for truth, people believe in many strange and difficult-to-defend beliefs. Throughout history, the complete irrationality of the world has led some groups to worship strange gods, to sacrifice their fellow humans in the hopes of a good harvest, and to mutilate themselves and others for artificially constructed notions of beauty. The world is a bizarre place that is difficult to make sense of, and it only gets stranger by the day.

People are often looking for answers. While the world seems to make little sense, people long for the solutions necessary to make themselves and their families safe and economically stable. However, they sometimes let themselves be convinced of things that are impossible. It is often not their fault. Modern civilization is so rife with contradictions and inconsistencies that sometimes the absurd is the only thing that makes sense. For example, for decades, in the African American community in the US, anti-medical establishment beliefs were cultivated based on the idea that they offered unethical experiments and fake treatments to men in the African-American community. To this day, there is a strained relationship between the African-American community and the healthcare industry because the belief persists that the medical industrial complex conducted decades' worth of unethical experiments without participants' knowledge. This belief is so widespread and so ingrained in the community that when Jordan Peele made the 2017 Film *Get Out*,[1] it became a huge success. An element of the film that resonated with audiences was the way the film dealt with this fear of medical experiments done on Black men without the participants' knowledge. This fear proved to be a significant concern for vaccine campaigns throughout the COVID-19 pandemic where celebrities and community leaders had to mobilize to create acceptance in the Black community in America.[2]

This belief in a secretive group of powerful people lying to a group of less powerful people has become a popular narrative among individuals often described by themselves and others as truthers, skeptics, and conspiracy theorists. Other similar theories include the belief that the CIA used mescaline, cocaine, marijuana, and LSD to brainwash people; the theory that they orchestrated false flag incidents in Iraq and Vietnam to hoodwink a populace into supporting an unpopular war; and that US drug companies and manufacturers exploit people in developing nations in Africa and South America by intentionally infecting them with HIV and other sexually transmitted diseases. Ideas like this persist in the US and elsewhere despite efforts from the medical industry, the news media, and governments to dispel and disprove these ideas. Citizens have been told the CIA cannot legally operate on US soil and would not violate that dictum for fear of repercussions.

Major news outlets like the *New York Times* and CNN have diligently and deliberately outlined how the US ship The USS Maddox in the Gulf of Tonkin was attacked by Vietnamese combatants,[3] how Saddam Hussein's soldiers took babies out of incubators in Kuwaiti hospitals and brutally tossed them onto the floor to die,[4] and how later, Hussein was accumulating yellow cake uranium to construct weapons of mass destruction.[5][6] [7] The problem is these irrational and unfounded fears—Black men being experimented upon, the MKUltra program, false flag incidents used as a justification for invasion—are true and are now noncontroversial opinions that mainstream news outlets and politicians admit to and even discuss in public.

Robert McNamara admitted in his interview with Errol Morris that the Gulf of Tonkin incident was fake.[8] Nayirah al-Ṣabaḥ was later revealed to be the daughter of a Kuwaiti ambassador whose story of incubator babies being killed was entirely fiction designed to alter the opinions of the US public.[9] There were no weapons of mass destruction in Iraq in 2003 and even the former head of the FBI, James Comey, admitted as much in his book[10]; the former speaker of the house even revealed they knew it to be true.[11] We also now know, thanks to the work of Seymore Hersh, that project MKUltra was a real program, heavily funded and widely in use.[12] It was probably responsible for the death of thousands. Barack Obama apologized to Guatemala for the US government's role in infecting people in its population with STDs to study the effect of penicillin.[13] Finally, the Tuskegee experiments[14] and the exploitation of Henrietta Lacks[15] are two well-known examples of African Americans being exploited and unethically experimented upon without the knowledge or consent of the individuals subject to the experiments. African Americans were also but one subgroup of individuals targeted by the MKUltra experiments, which also affected those in mental health facilities, in prisons, and in the armed services.[16]

These are just a few examples of suspicions and theories that people had, which turned out to be true. It recalls the famous quote (often misattributed to Mahatma Gandhi) from union leader Nicholas Klein in 1914, who said, "First they ignore you. Then they ridicule you. And then they attack you and want to burn you. And then they build monuments to you." While at first, some claims seem completely outrageous or even impossible, with time, more evidence has emerged that has revealed these extraordinary claims to be true. The few incidents mentioned here are but a few of the list of "outrageous" beliefs, which later turned out to be true. The list is very long, and it includes things like Nazi scientists being secretly incorporated into the space race,[17] the assassination of Martin Luther King Jr. whose assassin was exonerated in a civil case,[18] the Iran-Contra Affair,[19] and the famous "business plot" exposed by Smedley Butler, who was hired by wealthy industrialists to stage a coup and depose Franklin Roosevelt.[20]

It is not hard to notice a few other theories that turned out to be true when it comes to the COVID-19 pandemic. Most notable is perhaps the early theory that the disease that spread from Wuhan China was leaked from the Wuhan lab of Virology rather than from the Chinese wet markets. As will be touched on later in the book, this debate was ferocious and proponents of the former theory were silenced and punished throughout 2020 and 2021, until in 2022, when it became a commonplace and a noncontroversial opinion to entertain the lab leak as a viable theory.

As a reader, you might wonder why this is all being brought up. This history of misinformation and debate is being brought up to prime a reader for what follows. Even the most open-minded readers might find the information in this book difficult to believe, outlandish, or even offensive. It is important that each of the claims in the book is measured against these formerly dismissed theories that later turned out to be true.

The LIBOR scandal,[21] The Iran-Contra Affair, the Watergate Scandal,[22] and the PRISM spying ordeal[23] considered on their own merits, sound impossible, but each one has proven to be true. While any inquisitive and thoughtful person should check each claim they come across to ensure its veracity, it is important that claims not be dismissed immediately because of their unlikelihood. Extraordinary claims require extraordinary evidence, but this is true both of fringe beliefs and the mainstream narrative. This book aspires to that level of evidence with dozens of footnotes to articles from mainstream news sources, independent outlets, university studies, and books. It strives to provide information that offers the level of extraordinary proof required to prove the extraordinary claims made in this book.

Chapter 1

Has There Ever Been True Democracy?

Before we understand the present, we must understand the past. This chapter will briefly consider the history of governance and its effect on the populace. We will see how state control is inversely proportional to personal liberty and how that has been true throughout known human history. We will start with hunter-gatherers and see how they evolved into socially stratified agrarian societies and how those societies' ruling systems, irrespective of food and security concerns, expanded to achieve higher and higher levels of control. In this chapter, certain preconceived notions will be challenged. We think of modern democracy as the culmination of previous methods of leadership, but that assumption does not take into account all the twists and turns of human history. It does not consider the thorny complexities of rule and the many critiques of how power is acquired and maintained in the modern world.

We will ask complex questions about democracy and representative governments, and discuss how those groups interact with the populations they are supposed to represent. The patterns that emerge throughout human history may be surprising.

From Hunter-Gatherer to Domesticated Serf

The story of humankind is thorny. We perceive the story through the lens of progress and evolution whilst being mindful that our history belongs to that of the "victor." By this we mean the history they teach us and is widely accepted is rarely challenged. There is mounting evidence that a "lost" civilization, which had secret and forbidden knowledge, might have been erased from the annals of history; various books by Graham Hancock[1] and Marco M. Vitago's excellent *The Empires of Atlantis, the Origins of Ancient Civilizations and Mystery Traditions Throughout the Ages*[2] make for compelling evidence, which we will explore in further books of this series. For now, we will presume the accepted anthropological pedagogy of today reigns supreme. Looking back at early hunter-gatherer societies, it is as if we are seeing an unevolved version of our current society. It seems as if we are seeing uncomplicated people and, by comparison to the modern individual, the pre-agrarian human looks to be unsophisticated. But is that true? That is what all our history books tell us.

The story we are usually told is that ancient societies organized themselves around collecting berries and hunting game. Homo erectus, who sported a larger brain and shorter digestive system supporting an increase in the consumption of meat, appeared around 1.9 million years ago.[3] Homo erectus was a nomadic hunter, and these ancestors of ours organized their society around this form of food consumption. This continued through to the Neanderthals and the first appearance of anatomically modern humans. These groups were surprisingly egalitarian and developed cultural norms such as gathering for communal hearth time, burying their dead, and creating art. Once the game was overhunted and the bushes picked clean, these groups would move to a new location to avoid starvation.

However, a series of environmental changes led to a drastic change around 12,000 years ago. That drastic change coincided with the rise of organized governmental systems; it was a cataclysmic event called the Younger Dryas.

Around 10,000 BCE, the Neolithic Revolution began. Near the Middle East's Fertile Crescent, these groups began transitioning from hunting and gathering to farming. Once farming was developed as a viable alternative to hunting and gathering, these ancient tribes became more organized. In the Neolithic Age, or the Stone Age, people began to plant and harvest, replacing the earlier system of primarily hunting. This agricultural revolution was a drastic change because rather than establishing a symbiotic relationship with the land and the local flora and fauna populations, the pace of modern-day life was dictated by the proactive efforts of where to farm, when to farm, and how much to farm. This necessitated far more decisions to be made. When the need to protect the crops from rivals and animals was factored in, the rise of a decision-making class made sense. Leaders started making decisions on behalf of the group.[4] The change may have precipitated these power-coalescing systems, or it may have been a product of them.[5] Either way, history tells us that these systems of government were necessary and for the benefit and betterment of humankind, but were they?

This transition from a nomadic lifestyle to a more sedentary lifestyle took place asynchronously across the globe around 10,500 to 6,000 years ago.[6] In China, the cultivation of crops began around 9,000 BCE, while this did not occur in Mesoamerica until 7,000 BCE or in Africa until 5000 BCE.[5] With this new form of food acquisition came many changes, including a growth in population, the development of new tools, the domestication of animals, as well as new types of societal organizations. All these developments resulted in changes we still experience in our cultures today. If it were not for the Neolithic Age, we would not have had the Bronze Age, the Iron Age, or modern society as we know it (for better or worse[7]). While this period brought with it various technological developments and advancements, there has recently been a re-consideration of this period, since it also brought with it consequences such as a reduction of leisure time,[8] land disputes that led to war, environmental destruction, disease, and slavery.[9] With this agrarian-based society came another development that remains with us to this day—social stratification and the drastic increase of wealth disparity among members of the society.[10]

According to Mattia Fochesato and Samuel Bowles' study *Technology, Institutions, and Wealth Inequality Over Eleven Millenia*, "The key to understanding the evolution of economic inequality are changes in the distribution of political power, such as that which occurred due to the increasing domain of private property during the early Neolithic..."[11] With the Neolithic Age, we see drastic wealth disparities. The evidence presents itself to us archeologically as burial sites where the wealthiest and most powerful members of a society have ornate burial sites constructed that would require the labor of hundreds or thousands of men. This display of power, even in death, reveals the disparity in power and influence between the haves and have-nots of these societies.[12] The power of these elites is also evidenced in objects and artifacts like ornately designed vessels, weapons, armor, and jewelry. In only a few thousand years, societies went from being nomadic and having so few possessions that they had no choice but to be egalitarian, to societies where one individual could have orders of magnitude more wealth and privilege than someone else in their own community.

Looking back on the development of the societies that led to the modern stratification of today's society, we can learn something of ourselves from these ancient peoples. We can see the origins of our own problems and how power structures were designed, implemented, and exploited. So, what kinds of governments emerged to control and exploit people during this era? As agrarian societies emerged all over the world, governments developed to organize, maintain, and exploit the people of these societies. The Archaic Greek period, dating back to the 8th Century BCE, saw the rise of aristocratic oligarchies in the emergence of city-states. Japan established an emperor, while Rome had a monarch. China had a series of dynasties dating back to around 2070 BCE, where the governance was based on protecting the populace from rivals, and power was handed down through the generations rather than passing leadership on to capable successors. Egyptians, from 3000 BCE until well into the Common Era, were known for developing a hierarchy with the god-like Pharaoh at the top and the farmers and laborers at the bottom, toiling for the Pharaoh's benefit. Harappan, the civilization formed in the Indus Valley, had a centralized government around the same time as the Egyptians. This central government made itself responsible for urban planning and maintaining consistency in their bricks, weights, and pottery. The most ancient form of government emerged in Sumer in ancient Mesopotamia, located in modern-day Iraq. Sumer divided their settled area into a series of city-states governed by a religiously imbued ruler. They developed a law called the Code of Ur-Nammu.[13]

Ancient Sumerians, like these other civilizations, developed various elements of their society. They farmed, raised cattle, wove textiles, made advancements in building, carpentry, and pottery, and even fermented yeast to make beer.[14] They created schools, maintained written records, and wrote poetry and songs. They also exploited their labor for the benefit of their ruling class. The elites battled one another for control, and a series of power struggles upended the Sumerian way of life, paving the way for the Babylonians to take control of the area. Just like in so many cultures, the rise of governmental control led to an extension and intensification of the division of labor.

Types of Governments

It is relevant here to consider the prominent types of government. While modern governments have their roots in the ancient world, it was during the Enlightenment period that debates of modern governmental philosophies took shape, in particular Thomas Hobbes and the reaction to his monarchical notions by thinkers such as Locke, Montesquieu, and Rousseau. Hobbes perceived there to be a "social contract" between people. While people could live in a "State of Nature" where they would constantly be in conflict with others for resources, the cost of operating in a society was to "Lay down their nature and submit to the authority." [15] In Hobbes' case, he saw the monarch as the perfect embodiment of this social contract.

The Enlightenment Era thinkers of the late 1600s and early 1700s opposed and amended these notions as they discussed, debated, and designed the modern forms of democracy ushered in by the French and American Revolutions. Locke is famous for articulating the notion of "inalienable rights." He also saw the government's role as limited, as opposed to Hobbes' perception that the government was the embodiment of the law. Montesquieu favored a separation of powers to keep any one area of government from being too powerful. Rousseau advocated for the will of the people, wishing them to be imbued with the power of the sovereign. While all these thinkers agreed upon the existence of a social contract, they disagreed on how that social contract should manifest in society.[16] The problem they all faced came down to "who gets to decide." It is a debate that has been raging since there was anything to decide.

Monarchies into Democracy

Monarchies emerged out of paternalistic societies with the idea that certain members of a clan are more equipped to lead than others and have privileges other members of the clan do not. These privileges are granted by the group or perceived to be granted by a divine entity of some sort. Monarchies changed with the emergence of the idea of egalitarianism, where all would be equal under the law. They changed even further with the advent of the constitutional monarchy. This change—famously brought about by the Whigs in England but emerging in other places as well—introduced a parliament into the governance of a state, relegating the monarchy to a collaborative or purely ceremonial role.[17]

The common perception is that monarchies rob the rights of the ruled by imbuing all power to the monarch, but some, like Sam Branthoover, have questioned this logic citing the fact that monarchs can maximize earning potential for themselves as well as their subjects because superstitious belief in the monarch's power seems to streamline transactions and mitigate theft and graft.[18] This mirrors the work of Hans-Hermann Hoppe, who asks similarly provocative questions.

Democracies All the Way Back to Serfdom Again

The work of Hans-Hermann Hoppe has famously argued, in his essay "From Aristocracy to Monarchy to Democracy," that our common understanding of the evolution of government is incorrect. He aligns himself with Hobbes in his view that everyone in the world is at odds with one another. This is not because of the state of nature, but rather to scarcity. "Men do not live in perfect harmony with each other. Rather, again and again, conflicts arise between them. And the source of these conflicts is always the same: the scarcity of goods."[19] His assessment concludes that modern democracy is not the "end point of history" as so many scholars like to frame it. In fact, Hoppe argues that a constitutional monarchy is freer and fairer than our current system of democracy. He sees this as true for several philosophical, economic, and practical reasons.

Hoppe does not argue that a monarchy is the best form of government. In fact, he argues for its superiority over democracy to display democracy's failings.

"What I have tried to show here is why all of this is not a historical accident, but something that was predictable. Not in all details, of course, but as far as the general pattern of development is concerned. That the ultimate error committed, leading to these deplorable results, was the establishment of a territorial monopoly of ultimate decision making, i.e., a State, and hence, that the entire history we are told and taught in schools and standard text-books, which presents democracy as the crowning achievement of human civilization, is just about the opposite of the truth."[20]

Whether or not you agree with Hoppe's assessment, he proves it is folly to assume the current system of governance is automatically the best one or the only plausible one. He objects to the notion of The State as a decider and The State as self-policing. He pokes holes in the current coalescence of democracy and capitalism and hopefully provokes the asking of certain questions like, *Why do we do things the way we do?* and *Cui bono?* (Who benefits?)[21]

Conclusion

Having considered the history of human organization and self-governance, and seen how it has evolved and mutated, certain questions remain. Indeed, this text is not situated as being able to provide a solution to the problems observed, but it is merely a tome by which these assessments can be considered. Looking at the history and emergence of democracy through the lens of state power, we can see a certain sinister volition emerge. It is crucial to retain the notion of such volition through the rest of this book, as the disguise of acting for the public good will be a common theme throughout. As Hoppe points out, democracy is taught in schools as the end of a long metamorphosis. It is as if democracy is a butterfly that emerged naturally over time from the pupa that is human need, desire, and well-being. Democracy is presented as the natural outgrowth of the family and of humanity's need for safety and shelter. In the following chapters, we will see how countries are formed around ideas that benefit the elites of those countries, and how globalists usurp sovereign states via supranational organizations, all in the name of democracy.

Organizations such as the World Health Organization (WHO), Organization for Economic Co-operation and Development (OECD), Bank for International Settlements (BIS), International Monetary Fund (IMF), United Nations Educational, Scientific and Cultural Organization (UNESCO), the World Intellectual Property Organization (WIPO) and other organizations of this type, present themselves as democratically run organizations who operate according to some semblance of law, though they supersede state sovereignty, and are rarely governed by any law. They capitalize on and exploit international law, as much as it exists, to manipulate states to their will. Not only that, but they also act as a web of overlapping members and joint ventures to strengthen their own power and each other's to the detriment of the populace they are supposed to serve.

Chapter 2

The Great "United Nations"-Reset

The United Nations (UN) is perceived in society in a certain way. It established itself and its reputation worldwide as a purveyor of peace and justice and as a source of good. It has long been pointed to as an example of co-operation and prestige. Representatives from the UN are often portrayed in the media as the opposite of corrosive and exploitative corporations. They are pitted against spokespeople for weapons manufacturers in talking head segments, and they comment about the harm and destruction of dangerous and tyrannical regimes. The UN has instant name recognition as the organization on the side of the citizen, on the side of peace, and on the side of justice. Its real goals, however, do not always match that perception.

Often the very organizations and governments they are pitted against in the news media are actually working with the organization. Most people would be surprised by how much overlap there is between global corporations, dictatorial governments, and the UN leadership.

This chapter will examine the history of the UN and its various endeavors. It will also look at the organizations the UN is working with to pursue certain surprising endeavors.

The UN: Perception vs. Reality

In the media, The UN is often presented as a positive organization concerned with fairness and equality. It goes all the way back to Stanisław Lem's 1961 novel *Solaris,*[1] where the UN is perceived by alien life as the representative of humanity. The trend continues in the 1966 Batman[2] movie, where Batman's villains attack the UN, and the heroes must rescue them. In that children's movie, the UN is presented as such an unassailable paragon of truth and justice that it attracts the allyship of superheroes. Similarly, the UN is presented in films such as *Live and Let Die* (1973)[3] in the James Bond Franchise and Marvel's *Captain America: Civil War* (2016)[4] as an unbiased mediator between parties and an international metric for good. This is the image the UN would like to present to the world, but its actions do not always align with it. Their stated goals, according to their vision statement, are lofty, grand, and ambitious.

In accordance with the provisions of its Charter, the United Nations is committed to human progress and the preservation of the environment—our collective home. As we all know, our primary mandate, as prescribed in Article 1 of the Charter, is to "maintain international peace and security, and to that end: to take effective collective measures for the prevention and removal of threats to the peace, and for the suppression of acts of aggression or other breaches of the peace." In this noble undertaking, cooperation, collaboration, unity and solidarity must be the light we should seek and follow.[5]

Beyond that flowery language and performative affection for humanity, there are a tremendous amount of influential people, and these people have designs on how to assert their will globally. As this chapter will show, these admirable goals do not always seem to be the prime focus of the people in the organization, nor the organization itself.

The UN is certainly not without its critics, of course. Perhaps the most popular critique of this global organization is found in the film *Hotel Rwanda* (2004).[6] In the film, their involvement in international conflicts is presented as toothless, and their representatives are helpless to interfere in mass slaughter and are often ignored by local populations. This take would have been endorsed by the likes of Richard Nixon, who called it "obsolete and inadequate" in how it handled the Cold War[7] and the Oil-for-Food Program.[8] Critiques are not limited to those outside of the organization either. By the UN's own admission, it "failed to protect thousands" during the Sri Lankan Civil War.[9] It also receives criticism, not unlike other global organizations like the failed League of Nations, for its threat to national sovereignty, most famously from French president Charles de Gaulle who referred to it as "le machin" (the thing).[10]

One of its most chilling critiques comes in the form of the debates surrounding population control, abortion, and eugenics. The United Nations Population Fund (UNFPA) is a controversial program that has been criticized and even denied funding by several US presidential administrations.[11] This critique is notable because it is found both in the fringes and in the mainstream. Also, it stands in stark opposition to the critique that the organization is essentially powerless, and instead, hints at the vast power of the organization to control populations.

These criticisms have varying degrees of validity, which we will explore in later chapters. The UN, as the population control accusations hint, will be shown to be not merely a referee in global conflicts, but an actor on that stage. The international organization will be not simply a space for debate and resolution, but a global cabal compelling complicity. Believing this group is without options for solving global crises is perhaps one of the most dangerous mistakes a citizen can make.

Agenda 21, Agenda 2030 and Beyond

There is one critique, however, that has yet to gain the same level of traction in the mainstream media. It is a critique that overshadows all other critiques of the organization. From eugenics to individual cases of corruption, one UN effort contends for their most egregious sin and their most dangerous overreach. It is called Agenda 21.

Agenda 21 is a document initially drafted in 1992. The UN held a now infamous meeting in Rio de Janeiro, Brazil. The meeting was also known as the "Earth Summit," and it was ostensibly created as a plan to achieve sustainable growth as the 21st century dawned. This was the alleged reason for the name "Agenda 21." They created it as a series of recommendations, particularly for countries overtaxed by population and/or resource management problems. The plan, which is extant, is supposed to be a means to reign in growth and stave off the perils of overpopulation. The UN calls this agenda "nonbinding," thus reinforcing its reputation as "a damned debating society," as Nixon called it.[12]

The objectives of Agenda 21 are presented as elegant and ethical solutions to complex problems made by benevolent decision-makers. The stated goals of Agenda 21 include "Social and Economic Dimensions" as well as "Conservation and Management of Resources for Development."[13]

Under these two categories, the UN outlines various goals of the plan. These goals include sustainable development in developing countries, combating poverty, promoting human health, protecting the atmosphere, the oceans and freshwater supply, and the safe management of various types of waste. They outline the stated goals in a 350-page document, which is made available on the UN's website.[14]

Since the two-week conference in 1992, the agenda has evolved. The UN General Assembly has convened on these topics several times since its inception to assess the status of Agenda 21. These sessions occurred in 1997 (Rio+5), in 2002 (Rio+10), and then again in 2012 (Rio+20). The UN used these summits to reassess the original goals, review compliance, amend the original goals, and progress the agenda to new echelons.[15]

In 2015, the United Nations General Assembly adopted seventeen inter-linked global goals. These goals have considered the previous changes to the geopolitical landscape, the environment, and the adoption of the original principles. This new evolution takes Agenda 21 to the next stage as it hones and pushes forward many elements of the ideas devised in the 1990s. These seventeen "sustainable development goals" are listed below.

- GOAL 1: No Poverty

- GOAL 2: Zero Hunger

- GOAL 3: Good Health and Well-being

- GOAL 4: Quality Education

- GOAL 5: Gender Equality

- GOAL 6: Clean Water and Sanitation

- GOAL 7: Affordable and Clean Energy

- GOAL 8: Decent Work and Economic Growth

- GOAL 9: Industry, Innovation, and Infrastructure

- GOAL 10: Reduced Inequality

- GOAL 11: Sustainable Cities and Communities

- GOAL 12: Responsible Consumption and Production

- GOAL 13: Climate Action

- GOAL 14: Life Below Water

- GOAL 15: Life on Land

- GOAL 16: Peace and Justice Strong Institutions

- GOAL 17: Partnerships to Achieve the Goal[16]

This new phase of the agenda is known as Agenda 2030 and has more to do with implementation than previous iterations. Implementation will come to be the most alarming harbinger. According to a study by Cambridge University Press, the UN is frustrated at the speed of the implementation and is trying to increase the speed and the efficacy of compliance by utilizing "subnational authorities at the regional (federal states, provinces, regions) and local levels (cities, municipalities), along with corporate actors, such as individual businesses or business associations, and civil society, including nongovernmental organizations and community groups."[17] The plan is only accelerating, and it is doing so at a "subnational" level, which is an admission of its intention to circumvent autonomy.

Over 170 countries signed off on this plan, including the US, the UK, Canada, most of Europe, and many African, Middle Eastern, and Asian countries. Since its inception, the G20 nations have repeatedly cosigned and pledged compliance with this plan.[18] The number of nations participating has only grown. The agenda has transcended from the mere idea stage and is now being implemented at an ever more rapid rate. The evolutions continue with the United Nations Environment Program (UNEP) put into practice in 2022, bringing with it many new attempts to control the resources used by involved nations with a plan for net-zero carbon by 2050.[19] The evolutions will continue beyond this with Agenda 2050 already in the works.[20]

Is Agenda 21 Good or Bad?

Why is this a problem? What is wrong with a group of global actors meeting to address anticipated problems and issues of the coming century? Who would oppose good health and the end to poverty? In a world beset upon by war, famine, and inequality, shouldn't someone be paying attention to how resources are used and how they are divided? If you listen to the warnings of the representatives from the UN, they have you believe that the use of fossil fuels will lead to war, famine, rising sea levels, and the type of post-apocalyptic future that is often only depicted in science fiction movies (the same movies where the UN is perceived as the mouthpiece of humanity). This is the justification the UN uses for asserting its control.

The scarier the doomsday scenario they lay out, the more likely they are to get people to go along with their plans. The problem is, to make progress with their goals, they have to infringe upon individual liberty.

It is undoubtedly a significant leap from climate-concerned global recommendations to a dictatorial, one-world government. After all, according to UNESCO, the UN focuses heavily on making sustainable development a top priority. They use the definition of sustainable development found in the 1987 Brundtland Commission Report. The report defines sustainable development as "development that meets the needs of the present without compromising the ability of future generations to meet their own needs."21

The source of the problem begins with the Brundtland Commission. According to Christian Gomez, "The Brundtland Commission was named after its chairwoman, Gro Harlem Brundtland, who at the time was beginning her tenure as vice president of the Socialist International (1986 to 1999)."22 So, we have an ever-expanding global organization setting agendas for how resources will be acquired and used over the next century, and they set that policy based on the goals of a self-described socialist. This is where the erosion of personal liberty and the elimination of private property begins.

Socialism is far from communism, some might argue. Scandinavian social programs are ushered in democratically, and a party affiliation does not necessarily indicate any sort of nefarious attempt to infringe on the personal freedoms of citizens of Western nations. This may be true, but to fully understand how individual liberty will be circumvented, how sovereign nations will be subjugated, and how regulations will justify international power grabs, we must discuss The Club of Rome.

The Club of Rome

While Nixon was calling The UN a "debate club," The Club of Rome was passing itself off as one. It was formed in Italy by the disciples of Thomas Malthus, the 18th-century economist whose primary concern was population growth outpacing agricultural production. The primary goal of these Malthusians was to discuss what they considered the leading problems of the age. Aurelio Peccei and Alexander King brought in thinkers from various fields from all across the globe, including David Rockefeller, to consider a system of meta-problems the likes of which all problems emerge, or what they called "the problematic." Since 1968, the group has released numerous books, pamphlets, and documents on climate catastrophe, overpopulation, and food crises—the most important of which is a 1972 tome called *The Limits to Growth.*[23] With these missives, they come to the now famous conclusion that maintaining the environment should control the discourse around global endeavors.

"In searching for a common enemy against whom we can unite, we came up with the idea that pollution, the threat of global warming, water shortages, famine and the like, would fit the bill. In their totality and their interactions, these phenomena do constitute a common threat which must be confronted by everyone together."[24]

It seems, by this quote, the focus of their efforts could have been anything. They could have chosen nuclear war, the emergence of a supervirus, or even an attack by space aliens. It did not seem to matter whether this threat was real, only that it was plausible and sufficiently dire. This quote reveals the efforts of the Club of Rome to be a mere calculation. It suggests that their work is simply propagandistic, rather than truthful and informative.

This effort to use sustainability as a justification for enacting policy has become the basis of so many global efforts. The Club of Rome, in its assessment of the world's problems, has connected itself to various powerful groups and individuals. These groups include, but are not limited to, Dutch Prince Bernhard's 1001 Nature Trust, The World Wildlife Fund (WWF), and the International Union for the Conservation of Nature. These groups are used as slush funds, lobbying outlets, and PR cover for the more controversial goals of the people in these groups. The people involved included Prince Phillip, Duke of Edinburgh, the aforementioned Prince Bernhard of Denmark, and scion of a pro-eugenicist family, Sir Julian Huxley, whose brother Aldous, famously wrote the dystopian novel, *A Brave New World*, which is now interpreted not as a warning, but as a suggestion. Joanne Woiakm, in a 2007 paper for *The Public Historian* entitled "Designing a Brave New World: Eugenics, Politics, and Fiction," said, "His brave new world can therefore be understood as a serious design for social reform, as well as a commentary about the social uses of scientific knowledge."[25] Again, the effort was made to ensure these endeavors seem anodyne, with a bent toward the benefit of nature and thereby humanity, while they were meant to serve the elite institutions who funded and orchestrated their creation.

Meanwhile, these groups were infused with Malthusian intent. While Huxley was founding these groups meant to preserve nature, he was also the president of the British Eugenics Society. This makes sense when you realize the groups intended to replace the old paradigm of "saving humanity from empire" with the new paradigm of "saving nature from humanity."[26] Their organizations' emblems were colorful, and they featured pictures of leaves and pandas, but their members, like Maurice Strong, slipped easily from founding a chapter of the Club of Rome, to heading up the WWF, to setting policy within the UN.

Maurice Strong established the Canadian branch of the Club of Rome. He also spoke at the 1992 UN Conference in Rio de Janeiro and was one of the main contributors to the Agenda 21 document.[27] The Club of Rome will come up again and again in discussions on the UN, the WEF, and the Great Reset, both in terms of the collaboration between the groups' members and in the philosophy these groups share. The plan to use the threat of climate change in forcing compliance will come up again.

Conclusion

It has long been the goal of elites from the world over to create a global, hegemonic power. The seats at the top have been established for a long time. In November 2022, Emmanuel Macron indicated that "We need a single global order."[28] This echoes the sentiments of US President George H. W. Bush, who revealed in 1990 that "Out of these troubled times, our fifth objective — a new world order—can emerge..."[29] The coalescing of power has been a constant theme of neoliberal thinkers, leaders, and academics over the past century. This includes Milton Friedman, whose seminal text *Capitalism and Freedom*[30] has become the basis for neoliberal economics and the justification for globalism for decades, as well as the work of people like Henry Kissinger[31] and Gordon Brown.[32]

If the global elites are going to take steps toward a global order, the infrastructure is already in place. The UN is a worldwide organization with a long history of ignoring sovereignty. Agenda 21 (and its extension Agenda 2030) is an effort by the UN to utilize the public's awareness of climate change to roll back individual freedoms, and to acquire control of resources such as land, wealth, freshwater, and personal property. The goal is to subvert democracy and ignore elected officials to exert control. Various tools, including a debt-based economy, land use regulations, taxes, and propaganda, will all be used to employ this plan. The rest of the book will explore the other organizations colluding with the UN to enact such policy, and how attempts are being made to justify it.

Chapter 3

The Road to Davos

Certainly, public perception and political will are important things to cultivate when accumulating power. As discussed in the previous chapter, the UN connects to many other groups, like the Club of Rome, the WWF, and the 1,001 Nature Trust. These groups use climate change and sustainability to whip public discourse as a vector for change. Nothing can happen, however, without control of the money supply. Because of this, there is one group that is of particular interest, and one which should be explored in greater detail. It is a group with various connections to the previously mentioned groups as well as others. That group is the World Economic Forum (WEF).

Origins of the WEF

The WEF has its origins in Switzerland in 1971. It was not called the WEF at that time. It was originally called the European Management Fund.[1] The creators called it "The Forum" for short, as if it was the only one ever to be, and the only one that would ever be needed. The location for this forum, Davos, Switzerland, is just as ostentatious as the name. This is the same location as the setting for Thomas Mann's epic 1924 novel *The*

Magic Mountain,[2] which is a meditation on Bourgeois society, illness, and death, and takes place at a sanatorium, where various strange rituals are performed by the wealthy attendees. The Forum has been held annually since 1971, acting as a platform for various ideas and agendas to be put forward, often prompting debate amongst the public, and sometimes even among members of the organization.[3]

By 1987, the group had changed its name from the European Management Forum to the more ambitious WEF, and it had established itself as either an agenda-setting organization or simply a ski vacation for the uber-wealthy, depending on whom you ask. They waved off the former supposition as paranoia,[4] while the latter image was sometimes cultivated by the group itself.[5] This downplaying of the organization's efficacy has shades of the UN's and the Club of Rome's efforts to present themselves as merely "debate societies."

To understand what the organization seems to accomplish, and for what reason, the group's actions, alliances, and operational history must be observed. The group's origins must be understood. The organization's goals and complicated history cannot be extricated from its founder, Klaus Schwab.

Klaus Schwab

Schwab earned a Doctorate in Engineering at ETH (Swiss Federal Institute of Technology) and a Doctorate in Economics at the University of Fribourg. He also acquired a Master of Public Administration at Harvard where, by his own admission, he fell under the tutelage of Dean George Baker, Kenneth Galbraith, and Henry Kissinger.[6] These people, and his time at Harvard, would shape the rest of his life. It was at Harvard that

Schwab would participate in Kissinger's "International Seminar of the Summer School," which was set up by, and received at least $135,000 in funding, from the CIA.[7] The Summer School and Seminar has since cultivated a reputation as being a CIA operation for dictating global policy. Indeed, Henry Kissinger's mentor, William Yandell Elliott, used the school to indoctrinate prominent international figures. Schwab was not the only international power player to come through the program. Various figures of international renown had their start in the international seminar, including Yasuhiro Nakasone, Yigal Allon, and Pierre Trudeau. Yandell decrees that:

"The Summer School and Seminar, as specified by its charter, brought 'persons between the ages of 26 and 45 who are on the verge of reaching positions of leadership in their own countries,' including parliamentarians, academics, and others from around the world, in order to shape postwar strategic, educational, and cultural policy."[8]

Klaus Schwab would reuse this model later when putting together the WEF's Young Global Leaders program.

Schwab would become a professor at the University of Geneva, but he was not to become exclusively an academic. It was in 1971, at the inaugural European Management Forum, Klaus organized the European Management Symposium, which was "a major success, yielding a profit of 25,000 Swiss francs, which went to endow the European Management Forum."[9] It was the success of this first meeting that allowed for the founding of the European Management Forum and, eventually, the WEF. The organization makes no secret that Keynesian economist Kenneth Galbraith and Herman Kahn—a man known as the "real life Dr. Strangelove"[10]—were among its first organizers, speakers, and participants, or that Schwab was an acolyte of these powerful and controversial figures in international political history.

These three men (Kissinger, Khan, and Galbraith) were well known for the way they stepped out of the confines of the accepted knowledge base of their disciplines and relied on rhetoric to win arguments and get their way, rather than scholarship, veracity, and data.

"Other mainstream economists, such as Scott Gordon and Robert Solow, also pointed out fundamental problems with his [Galbraith's] conclusions—problems Galbraith never seriously grappled with. Instead, he focused on the witty epigram. As one critic pointed out, Galbraith's main form of argument for key assumptions in his model of the economy was a 'vigorous assertion.'"[11]

Kissinger cultivated a similar image. His mentor Fritz Kraemer would teach Kissinger "not to emulate 'cleverling' intellectuals and their bloodless cost-benefit analyses... Only if you do not 'calculate' will you really have the freedom which distinguishes you from the little people."[12]

Herman Kahn was a firebrand and an iconoclast in his field, hyping up the threat of nuclear war and proposing scenarios, and considering tactics so purposefully outrageous they stunned people even in his own field. They were movers of opinion in their own circles and in the world at large. It is not surprising these men would use think tanks and international forums to dictate public thought, affect policy, and indoctrinate leaders the world over. They would rely on pomp, circumstance, and shock and awe to convince their audience they were correct, rather than relying on data and logic.

These men always seemed to find themselves involved in various panels and groups, the intention of which was to help shape European policy. "All three men were members of the Council on Foreign Relations, the American branch of the Anglo-American imperialist 'Round Table' movement... and they often popped up in various European think tanks and panels to dictate the course of discussion."[13] "They would also seek to impose global power structures shared by big business, the political elite, and academia."[14]

It is out of this group of men the WEF was birthed. Klaus Schwab, shaped and molded by Harvard and a group of bombastic international influencers, formed an international council of his own. He took what he gleaned from the Harvard International Seminar and began his work of promulgating a particular worldview. From cross-pollinating with other powerful groups to developing acolytes to send into prominent positions in the world through the William Yandell Elliott and Henry Kissinger-influenced Young Global Leaders program, Schwab used his education well.

The Young Global Leaders Program

The WEF calls the Young Global Leaders program "the voice for the future and the hopes of the next generation" and presents the program as a glorified academic conference, or a highly exclusive social network; however, in its ranks are people who have later found themselves in highly influential positions able to affect global outcomes and the international landscape. It has become a means by which the WEF can instill its ideas in people who can implement them. These leaders include Angela Merkel, Vladimir Putin, and Tony Blair. The ranks also include Justin Trudeau, who is the son of Pierre Trudeau, the former Prime Minister of Canada, and a fellow participant with Schwab of Harvard's International Seminar.[15]

The Young Global Leaders are not limited to economics or politics, as many Silicon Valley mavens such as Mark Zuckerberg, Chad Hurley (co-founder and CEO of YouTube), and Josh Silverman (CEO of Skype) have all been involved in the program as well.[16]

The Young Global Leaders program is used to indoctrinate young people before they enter the stratosphere of public life. The WEF plucks young and ambitious people from universities and the business world, imparts the mission of the WEF upon them, and then places them into the highest echelons of power. They do this by their own admission. In an interview,[17] Klaus Schwab explained how proud he was of the program as a means to install people sympathetic to the mission in positions of power.

"We penetrate the cabinet. So yesterday I was at a reception for Prime Minister Trudeau, and I know that half of his cabinet, or even more than half of his cabinet, are actually Young Global Leaders."[18]

Klaus designed the program to create public-private partnerships in the tech, energy, and consumer goods spaces, thus infusing the WEF's doctrine into every corner of commerce. "The ultimate consequence of both public–private partnerships and these target areas is the creation of a tyrannical social contract in which the individual has become subordinated to these powerful interests."[19]

This is not at all unlike the program from which Schwab is himself a product, Henry Kissinger's International Seminar at Harvard University. The Young Global Leaders program and Kissinger's program have many similarities. "Originally, the United States created these secretive youth organizations with the aim of targeting potential future European leadership candidates. Yet soon, no country in the world would be safe from possible CIA-sponsored political infiltration."[20]

The International Seminar received its funding from various CIA money laundering foundations. The CIA has a long history of establishing organizations that then award money to certain groups or entities for "research" or "outreach" but ostensibly do the CIA's bidding, whether or not the participants know it. A few organizations used to fund Kissinger's program include The Asian Foundation, The Farfield Foundation, and The American Friends of the Middle East.

Kissinger notably had a hand in developing the Young Global Leaders. In 1992, Kissinger and Klaus' alma mater, Harvard, awarded Klaus Schwab $1 million dollars through a foundation called the Dan David Foundation, which Henry Kissinger controlled. In a way, Kissinger was recreating his international seminar via one of his prized pupils.

Once this structure was in place, the ideas of the WEF could spread. While the CIA-funded endeavor from the 1960s was once concerned with the overreach of communism and perceived threats to the American Empire, the Young Global Leaders program is now, ironically, pushing forth an agenda that undermines the principles of capitalism. A central tenet of the WEF and its many devotees is stakeholder capitalism. Indeed, the Wallstreet Journal called Schwab an "evangelist" for the idea,[21] but what is stakeholder capitalism, and why is it so important to Schwab and the WEF?

Stakeholder Capitalism

Stakeholder capitalism is Klaus Schwab's pet theory. It maintains that "customers, suppliers, employees, shareholders, and local communities" all hold a stake in the capitalistic system.[22] Schwab states that this is a way to connect the globe in its fight against resource depletion and climate change by relying on compromise among shareholders to achieve balance. Detractors claim that stakeholder capitalism is a PR maneuver for corporations to present themselves as thoughtful and inclusive.[23]

We can see this kind of public image manipulation in the way the Vatican has partnered with the WEF to create the Council for Inclusive Capitalism (CICV). The founder of the CICV, Lynn Forester de Rothschild, declared, "This council will follow the warning from Pope Francis to listen to 'the cry of the earth and the cry of the poor' and answer society's demands for a more equitable and sustainable model of growth."[24, 25] By positioning itself alongside a major religion, the WEF seems to be a compassionate organization. By adopting this seemingly inclusive approach to money management, the ever-beleaguered Catholic church launders its public image as an organization. It is a win for both organizations, but whom does it help beyond that?

At worst, the theory is not capitalism at all, and it is merely a means by which the powerful can circumvent national autonomy.

"WEF... will focus on how to accelerate 'stakeholder capitalism' and its cousin ESG (short for environmental, social, and governance), two related movements that diminish economic freedom, the key to prosperity, and push us closer towards a new brand of socialism."[26]

These ESG measures are essentially a means by which technocrats can put their thumb on the scale of free markets. Rather than consumers deciding what has value, the WEF will determine value, thus circumventing sovereignty, capitalism, and individual freedom.[27]

The ESG system has been compared to China's infamous social credit system, and the critiques of it are myriad. Essentially, the system is a reporting system where the environmental, social, and governance scores are tabulated and submitted as a social credit framework for sustainability reporting. The problem with this begins when we look at who will determine the value of each score. The answer will not be a surprise. The plan, according to Schwab, is to put corporations, banks, and financial institutions in control of these tools. This will heap even more power onto these organizations as market forces will react to their whims, rather than the other way around. The closest analog would be if politicians got to decide how much each vote was worth. They could not be trusted with that power any more than a bank could be trusted with the power to determine a competitor's risk profile based on their social aptitude. It adds an element of subjectivity to economic valuations that threaten to subvert the basic building blocks of capitalism. The system ignores consumer valuation in favor of corporate and financial institution desires.[28]

Regardless of whether it is a socialist effort to subvert capitalism, a PR makeover of corporate greed or an earnest attempt to apportion resources ethically, it is a drastic shift in understanding how economies are constructed.

The WEF and the Great Reset

In June 2020, Schwab released a book-length plan for how to react to the COVID-19 pandemic from an economic standpoint. The book was called *COVID-19: The Great Reset.*[29] According to the marketing material of the book, it "is a guide for anyone who wants to understand how COVID-19 disrupted our social and economic systems, and what changes will be needed to create a more inclusive, resilient and sustainable world going forward."[30]

According to the BBC, the plan "explores how countries might recover from the economic damage caused by the coronavirus pandemic."[31] Most articles from the mainstream media are quick to explain away critiques of the plan by pointing at the purported intentions of the book. It is common for these articles to defend the book as an exploration, an investigation, or even a guide. What these critiques often lack is a substantive discussion of the recommendations found within.

The book is broken into three main parts, none of which are new talking points or strategies for the WEF. These strategies include cultivating a "stakeholder economy," using ESG (environmental, social, and governmental) metrics in a variety of ways, and implementing the innovations of the Fourth Industrial Revolution."[32]

The solutions posed in the book boil down to increasing surveillance, increasing the power of governments and their ability to tax their citizens, and decreasing individual liberty.[33] Schwab claims that to avoid a pandemic in the future, "biosurveillance" is necessary. He also claims that "incentives" will encourage citizens to become stakeholders. By incentives, he means taxes and government intervention. This government intervention will eventually control consumption in a way dictated by elites of individual countries and perhaps, even by transnational organizations like the WEF and the UN.

While the mainstream media is quick to defend these plans, Schwab and his ilk are stating their goals outright. It's not a conspiracy; they use words like "reimagine" and "shape" to coerce readers into their web.[34] Schwab is putting forth the same ideas that were presented by the Club of Rome in the 1970s, just repackaged for a pandemic-wounded public. Schwab is a longtime proponent of the Club of Rome's predictions and policies.

In 1973, Schwab invited Aurelio Peccei to speak at the Forum at Davos. Peccei presented his report *Limits to Growth*. *Limits to Growth* is the chilling prediction based on a Massachusetts Institute of Technology model, which foresees an end to civilization due to a sudden population explosion combined with the collapse of energy resources. The report is famous for predicting "the most probable result will be a rather sudden and uncontrollable decline in both population and industrial capacity." It warns, "if the present growth trends in world population, industrialization, pollution, food production, and resource depletion continue unchanged, the limits to growth on this planet will be reached sometime within the next one hundred years." The philosophies of the WEF and the Club of Rome are aligned around this doomsaying.[35]

This is where the cross-pollinating ideas come together. Schwab is using a global crisis to push a policy that will necessitate less individual freedom and turn over control and decision-making responsibilities to elites like him. That is what the Great Reset argues for. The problems the Club of Rome, The UN, and the WEF identify are problems global in measure—problems like climate change, overpopulation, food production, and health—and their solutions involve mass submission to their will.

Conclusion

So where is this leading? It seems as if Schwab has an idea. He recently gave an interview where he praised China and called them "a role model for many countries."[36] Schwab claims to be enamored with China's modernization efforts over the past few decades. This model includes dictatorial rule, no tolerance for dissent or religious freedom, as well as a social credit system designed to reward submission and punish dissent, which is not unlike the ESG system Schwab has proposed in his writings on stakeholder capitalism. Schwab's mentor, Henry Kissinger, who is still advising on geopolitical maneuvers, commented in May 2022 about the US's relationship with China. "Henry Kissinger noted that the potentially adversarial aspect of the US-China relationship should be mitigated, and common interests should be pursued and upheld."[37] How quickly things progress from a Democratically elected Scandinavian socialist to an unelected elite deciding which businesses are rewarded and why.

Could Chinese-style rule be the end goal? It is unclear, though Schwab and his mentor, Kissinger, seem quite enamored with it. What is clear is the WEF has long-term plans, and these plans have to do with economic policy. It is hard to imagine that Schwab and other members of the ultra-elite are setting policies that will be detrimental to them. The agendas set at Davos benefit the people who set the agendas. If Schwab's book tells us anything, he is looking to capitalize on what he (and Nassim Taleb) call "Black Swan events," which are unexpected and game-changing incidents not unlike the collapse of the global housing market in 2008, any number of supply chain-disrupting natural disasters, or a global pandemic. Schwab and his organization want to capitalize on these events by expanding surveillance, expanding government, and demanding more austerity and sacrifice from citizens who are not a part of the elite Davos set.[38]

Chapter 4

The (not so) Great Reset

The UN and the WEF have now been exposed for what they really are, or at least for not being exactly what they purport to be. They are organizations with undisclosed funding sources and links to various organizations the world over. They are organizations with grand objectives and designs for acquiring power. These organizations are systematically achieving these objectives, but do they have anything to do with one another? It is one thing to be skeptical of the WEF and critical of the UN, but to see them as colluding in any meaningful way is taking a step toward paranoia. Isn't it?

While these two groups present as independent entities that seem to have little to do with one another, The Great Reset will be revealed as an endeavor that will link the two organizations in important ways, both public and private. This chapter reveals the conduits between the two organizations and how they have publicly intertwined themselves.

The Great Reset

The project, discussed in some detail in the previous chapter, is the WEF's attempt to change the way the world operates politically, economically, and environmentally. "The old systems are not fit anymore for the 21st century," Schwab said in an interview featured on the WEF's website.[1] Whether their goals for this are noble or nefarious remains to be seen.

We can find the first piece of information in determining this in the organization's involvement with Charles Philip Arthur George, now King Charles III. The WEF asked the then Prince of Wales to speak at the Forum in 2020. In the speech made on the 50th anniversary of the WEF, King Charles laid out a new initiative in the name of "Sustainability." King Charles III called the initiative a "sustainable markets initiative," but the problem he focused on in his speech was one of economics. "We need to evolve our economic model... it is not a lack of capital that is holding us back, but rather the way in which we deploy it. Therefore, to move forward, we need nothing short of a paradigm shift."[2]

In the name of sustainability, King Charles III would like to change the way money is spent paradigmatically. This sustainable markets initiative, funded by the WEF, intends to use climate change as an excuse to shape how markets operate. He does not go into detail about what economic and political tools will be employed to make this paradigm shift, but the implications have been enough to make even the mainstream media ask questions.

While most mainstream outlets are quick to establish a strawman argument, some are realizing what Ivan Wecke, for example, from Open Democracy has said,

"The idea of stakeholder capitalism and multistakeholder partnerships might sound warm and fuzzy, until we dig deeper and realize [sic] that this actually means giving corporations *more* power over society, and democratic institutions less... In practice, corporations become the main stakeholders, while governments take a backseat role, and civil society is mainly window dressing."[3]

Wecke has it right. That is what the Great Reset is meant to do. It is meant to evolve the power of supranational organizations like the WEF and the UN and to devolve the power of governments, whose main job is supposed to represent their citizens.

The 2021 World Summit on Food saw the UN working with the WEF and embracing the WEF's vision of a multistakeholder ecosystem to solve problems of world hunger. This is yet another example of the system of multilateralism (where democratically elected leaders come together to solve problems) is circumvented by Schwab's vision of stakeholder capitalism. According to Schwab and the WEF, this is a preferable alternative. Why is this troubling? The main concern has to do with the fact that if major public-private corporations are being tasked with solving problems related to climate change, global health, and world hunger, their solutions will often put their own interests first rather than the interests of the people of a particular region. Whereas corporations have long been known to insert themselves into political bodies via subterfuge and secret pacts, campaign financing, and outright bribes, this new system of stakeholder capitalism skips those steps and nakedly puts the corporate interests front and center.

Yuval Noah Harari

One of Klaus Schwab's main advisors and a key architect of the philosophy of stakeholder capitalism is a man named Yuval Noah Harari.[4] Like most involved with the WEF, the man has an impressive CV and an influential position. Harari is a graduate of the Hebrew University of Jerusalem with a doctorate from Jesus College at Oxford. He is a Professor of History at the Hebrew University of Jerusalem with articles in prestigious publications as wide-ranging as the *New York Times*, *The Economist*, *The Guardian*, *The Atlantic*, and *Nature* magazine. He is perhaps most well-known as the author of the 2011 book, *Sapiens: A Brief History of Humankind.*[5] The book occupies an interesting space in the constellation of popular thought with celebrities and public figures as diverse as Natalie Portman, Bill Gates, and Barack Obama praising and recommending the book.

The book outlines the history of humankind from a fresh perspective. This is not a unique thing in pop science circles. Every few years, a new book about the mind or the universe, or human history, tops nonfiction best-seller lists because of the book's ability to provide clever lines to upper-middle-class dilettantes who want to seem interesting at dinner parties. From Howard Bloom's *The Lucifer Principle*[6] to Brian Green's *The Elegant Universe*[7] to anything Malcolm Gladwell ever published, the template has been set. The major difference between these attempts at entertaining the hoi polloi with impressive terms and mostly true scientific factoids is the aforementioned writers do not have the ear of a man set to change the way economies function all across the globe for the next hundred years.

The book itself considers the friction between the natural sciences and social sciences. He worships at the altar of science and seems to use it as a justification for many atrocities. He considers scientific advancement to be inevitable and thus imperialistic, using logical fallacy to assert that if scientific advancement is inevitable, then empires are as well. Not only does Harari argue for the necessity of an empire, but he also says of the statement that "every people has a right to self-determination and should never be subject to the rule of another," is "deeply problematic." He ultimately concludes that imperial rule is "for your own good."[8] The thesis of the book is centered on how humanity's propensity for fiction and imagination has turned them from animals to gods. Indeed, becoming a god is a major element of the book. Harari sees humanity's creation of money, nations, and institutions as just the beginning. The book ends pseudo-apocalyptically with humans creating new subspecies of humans and ruling over them. Harari likes to claim that biological engineering, cyborg engineering, and AI engineering will ultimately allow humans to "upgrade themselves into gods."[9]

Darshana Narayanan, in her 2022 article for *Current Affairs Magazine*, described Harari thusly, "The best-selling author is a gifted storyteller and popular speaker. But he sacrifices science for sensationalism, and his work is riddled with errors."[10] Anthropologist C.L. Hallpike sums it up succinctly when he says, "It would be fair to say that whenever his facts are broadly correct, they are not new, and whenever he tries to strike out on his own, he often gets things wrong, sometimes seriously. So we should not judge *Sapiens* as a serious contribution to knowledge, but as 'infotainment'..."[11] Narayanan explains, however, in what ways Harari is essentially a charlatan, telling seductive stories of gene editing humans into perfection when his lofty predictions are almost entirely made up. François Chollet says about the possibility of algorithms attaining cognitive autonomy, "Today and for the foreseeable future, this is stuff of science fiction."[12]

This recalls Schwab's mentors, Henry Kissinger and Kenneth Galbraith, in that both these men were also described as compelling speakers who were similarly irresponsible with facts. Perhaps there is something Schwab finds appealing about a captivating salesperson. Troublingly, he is not the only one, as Mark Zuckerberg, the Managing Director of the IMF, the CEO of Axel Springer, and (in one of many overlaps between the UN and the

WEF) the UNESCO have all used Harari as a resource, or a consultant of sorts, to weigh in on the prevalent problems of the day.

Harari, in his book *Homo Deus,* calls himself a proponent of a new religion, "The Data Religion."[13] He foresees a future where decisions of groups, as well as individuals, will be made by algorithms. He considers this the destiny of humankind and perhaps the next step in human evolution. When his relationship with Schwab and UNESCO is considered, it makes sense in terms of the way the Great Reset is meant to synthesize humanity in a new way and use "a paradigm shift," as King Charles said, to change the relationship humans have with the world. It should not go without notice that this belief in algorithms to make decisions for huge groups of people removes individual freedom and autonomy from the equation.

While Harari's books are an instrumental aspect of his ability to spread information, he is also very drawn to televised interviews with the likes of Russell Brand and Jared Diamond, as well as multiple TED Talks. In these interviews and large-scale public speaking opportunities, he speaks extemporaneously, and one idea that comes up is that of Ayn Rand and her notion of the "useless eaters" mentality.

For those unfamiliar, Ayn Rand was born in Russia and was a victim of the Bolshevik Revolution, the horrors of which colored her perception of the world forever after. She famously crafted her philosophy of objectivism as a novelist and screenwriter. Her philosophy is a form of rational individualism that sees the achievement of the mighty as morally right based simply on the will to achieve and considers reason and logic as a moral imperative.[14]

Rand's Objectivism has some overlap with Harari's Data Religion and his will to become a god, in that both philosophies aspire to some greater objective truth, and both claim to be doggedly defined by reason. What could be more reasonable than measuring all the data and then determining the correct course of action after all? Inherent in both philosophies is a cold and unemotional eschewing of sentimentality. Both philosophies see the world as a place for the elite to rise to the top to be rewarded. In Harari's version, these perfect beings are even created with some form of eugenic-genetic editing. In Harari's version, he becomes a god.[15]

This is where he sees things heading, and he has found a way to appeal to the Davos elite. This future, where humanity makes itself into a god, is one he has sold to the most powerful. It is appealing since he situated them at the top and offered them some form of everlasting life and godlike power. He calls this future—or perhaps the present—the Fourth Industrial Revolution.

The Fourth Industrial Revolution

According to the WEF's website, the Fourth Industrial Revolution (4IR) is an outgrowth of the third.[16] While the First Industrial Revolution saw the rise of steam power and the second saw the world electrified, the third saw the world connected via the internet. The fourth will progress from the third and fuse data, technology, and interconnectivity to blur "the lines between the physical, digital, and biological spheres."[17]

This description is a little vague. It sings the praises of technological development while also hinting at a potential dark side. The WEF is particularly concerned with the benefits of an AI-driven economy, genome splicing, smart contracts, and e-government. It has gained many proponents who welcome and anxiously anticipate the coming revolution. These proponents include Matt Hancock (former UK Member of Parliament), who championed the idea with a government white paper[18] and several pro-4IR speeches,[19] and Mark Zuckerberg, whose metaverse is an attempt to accelerate society toward the inevitability of the 4IR. The 4IR is a technocrat's dream, but many warn of it as a potential nightmare.

Some see the coming changes as potentially devastating to the job market, with as many as fifty percent of current forms of employment disappearing, which would result in a drastic restructuring of how revenue and taxes are collected. This radical restructuring might result in new power grabs and forms of totalitarianism as authoritarians come to power to cope with the shifts in the global economy.[20] Other fears have to do with Central Bank Digital Currencies (CBDCs), health passports, and data transparency.[21] There are other critiques of this concept, and they come from an unlikely place.

To understand what the 4IR could be and how it might be implemented, we must return to Yuval Noah Harari. In March 2020, he published an article considering how to utilize coronaviruses for the betterment of mankind. In it, he discusses how the COVID-19 pandemic is accelerating the 4IR, and how it will equip humanity in new ways to deal with the ongoing crisis.

"As a thought experiment, consider a hypothetical government that demands that every citizen wears a biometric bracelet that monitors body temperature and heart rate 24 hours a day. The resulting data is hoarded and analyzed [sic] by government algorithms. The algorithms will know that you are sick even before you know it, and they will also know where you have been, and who you have met. The chains of infection could be drastically shortened, and even cut altogether. Such a system could arguably stop the epidemic in its tracks within days. Sounds wonderful, right?"[22]

Harari is coy in the article, presenting the opportunities of such technology as well as the downsides. Later in the article, however, Harari perhaps reveals his hand by making the pronouncement that so many in power do when they want to make a temporary change permanent, "Yet every crisis is also an opportunity."[23]

Not unlike how Aldous Huxley explored his ideas of Malthusian eugenics in his novel *Brave New World,* Harari is perhaps trialing ideas for how the world could look in the 4IR by trotting out these once-controversial notions. During times of crisis, people are notorious for ceding their freedoms and their autonomy in exchange for safety. Unfortunately, once those freedoms have been relinquished, they are rarely given back.

UN/WEF Partnership Framework

Now we come to how the UN and the WEF are working together to use sustainability as a justification to implement stakeholder capitalism during the crisis that is the 4IR. Why has the WEF been chosen as a UN partner for Agenda 2030 implementation?

In the summer of 2019, the WEF and the UN signed a new memorandum of understanding (MoU). The new WEF-UN agreement "creates a second special place for multinational corporations inside the UN." It has given rise to the fear that multinational corporations will have direct access to UN policymakers, thus gaining greater ability to assert their influence over issues of worldwide governance. Since the 2019 MoU between the UN and the WEF, the two groups have become overtly and inextricably linked, hinting that the UN is "quietly being turned into a public-private partnership."[24]

The agreement makes various promises of engagement between the two organizations, including a commitment by the secretary-general to deliver a keynote address at the WEF annual forum at Davos. The agreement also calls for the participation of senior UN staffs and the heads of programs, funds, and agencies to be involved in regional meetings hosted by the WEF, as well as a promise to cross-promote their joint events and endeavors. The MoU also calls for "build[ing] a shared understanding of sustainable investing... public commitments from the private sector to reach carbon neutrality by 2050..." and to "ensure inclusive and equitable quality education."[24] This is an explicit intertwining of the two organizations, the reality of which has been ridiculed by defenders of both the WEF and the UN. But this MoU between the two groups makes it clear they intend to work together. Not only that, but it also makes clear their intention to use "multistakeholderism" as the problem-solving mechanism du jour among those involved in the multilateral system. This is a threat to sovereignty, as the agreement sidesteps any sort of review process that governments affected by the agreement might otherwise conduct. As reported via Open Democracy, "the secretary-general joined the WEF in declaring in effect that multistakeholder groups with no formal intergovernmental oversight are a better governance system than a one-country-one-vote system."[24]

This ability to circumvent established systems of government to implement stakeholderism is the goal. They explicitly stated it to be the goal in this MoU. Despite words to the contrary, international groups seem to be solidifying and concentrating their power. In 2022, the G20 Leaders' Declaration detailed specific instructions to meet the UN Agenda 2030 goals "in a timely manner"[25] while the IMF, itself a hotbed of controversy worldwide, focused its G20 report on increasing sustainability.[26] Schwab was even seen in Bali, along with Bill Gates, while the G20 summit occurred.[27] While all of these forces congeal, their language becomes homogenized, and they continue to focus on the same ideas of sustainability as a justification for stakeholderism.

Conclusion

Even the staunchest defender of the UN could not deny they are overtly working hand-in-hand with the WEF. While it could be argued the goals of these explicit partnerships are meant to benefit people affected by coming changes to the socioeconomic landscape, it cannot be argued that they do not have an affiliation.

The collaboration is not merely in name. It is an active partnership, implementing the changes they have been talking about for some time. They act as if the 4IR is upon us and a foregone conclusion. For example, Bill Gates has become the biggest owner of farmland in the US.[28] Why is he doing this? He is a man obsessed with monopoly, anticipating the changes that will come during the 4IR. His farmland investment looks to be oddly well timed, considering the hugely detrimental environmental effects of the February 2023 Ohio train crash in East Palestine. Authorities burned off tanks of vinyl chloride into the atmosphere, thus creating highly carcinogenic dioxin compounds, which have a half-life of between 25-100 years and could poison the food chain for generations to come. Gates, whose words of praise appear above the title of Yuval Noah Harari's book, is anticipating the changes of the 4IR and is positioning himself as a sustainability partner for the coming decades. He is intimately familiar with the push to implement ESG scores; he is an ally of the UN and the WHO, and now that he has so much say in global health efforts, agriculture may be his next space to conquer. These are the kinds of moves the powerful make when they see change on the horizon. Gates' forays into sustainability, timely investments, and subsequent sales are not limited to agriculture, as we will see in the next few chapters.

Chapter 5

Pandemic or Scamdemic? Part 1

Was the COVID-19 pandemic really a pandemic, or was it a planned event that could be used as a stepping stone to condition the world population for the Agenda 2030 plans? What evidence do we have that prior to the pandemic, certain actors had not planned and engineered a SARS virus and subsequent release to scare the public into collectivist measures, and into thinking the only solution to surviving the pandemic was taking the mRNA vaccine? What does the patent trail tell us about the SARS-CoV-2 evolution?

As more cracks appear in the official narrative, it becomes more and more plausible that the pandemic was an orchestrated event used by the WEF to enact changes they had long planned. The pandemic offered the WEF a "rare opportunity," as they put it, to usher in the Great Reset. Klaus Schwab's book was authored, printed, and available by June 2020, only a few months after the pandemic was officially declared. The security state was utilized to push a prominent narrative and suppress dissent through various means. The groups who stood to gain were ready and waiting, positioning themselves as saviors the moment the problem began to emerge.

The more we learn, the more it seems these supranational organizations used the pandemic as an opportunity to act as a Trojan Horse for many of the policies and ideas the WEF had been toying with for years.

Where did the Vaccines Come From?

While the mainstream media focused on the need for vaccines to combat the growing threat of COVID-19, many scientists began ringing the alarm bell on the topic of vaccines, particularly in the realm of mRNA vaccines. One such scientist is a progenitor of the technology, Dr. Robert Malone. Since 2020, Malone has been pointing out the drawbacks and dangers of a vaccine he is intimately familiar with.[1] Malone was instrumental in the technology's development, though he claims his role has been drastically downplayed by others who helped to develop it. A particular issue he raises is with the technology itself. One of his major concerns is the governments' and health agencies' insistence upon using mRNA technology as the solution to the COVID-19 problem, while ignoring or suppressing other possible solutions. His fear, as well as the fear of many others, is that lionizing mRNA and familiarizing the public with it—normalizing its use—is itself the goal.

One early indicator that there is more to the story than the public was told is that the biotechnology firm Moderna had the first mRNA vaccines ready for use within two days of the SARS-CoV-2 genome sequence being made available. Against accepted protocols, Moderna concurrently conducted tests rather than sequentially to issue the vaccine under emergency use guidelines in the same year in which they created the vaccine. "Of course, vaccines are easy to create but creating one that is effective and safe is difficult," quipped *The Economist*.[2] We now know that Operation Warp

Speed occurred possibly at too fast a speed to ensure proper safety. The Food and Drug Administration (FDA) has since admitted oversight of clinical trials was "grossly inadequate."[3] This lack of oversight has led many to question if the right decisions were made, and if the safety of the public was actually the main goal of Pfizer and Moderna over profits.[4]

That Moderna could create a supposedly effective and safe vaccine in January 2020 without prior knowledge of the pandemic is suspicious. One reason for this could be that the virus and the vaccine existed before the public knew about either. That would account for all the breathless pronouncements of Moderna's "astonishing" speed. Indeed, the vaccine was manufactured and ready for Phase I clinical trials at the National Institute of Health in February 2020.[5]

Perhaps this is possible. Perhaps the global collective could indeed work around the clock and push out a vaccine this quickly. That still leaves open the possibility that the vaccine was designed and manufactured too quickly in a rush to capitalize on the immense profits a global pandemic seemed to offer.

There is still some debate about how real the threat of COVID-19 ever was or still is today. Much of the justification for how much money to allocate Operation Warp Speed, for whom to imbue with power, for how long and how fervently lockdowns should be implemented, came from the huge explosion of COVID-19 cases throughout 2020. We now know that many of those numbers were inflated by the use of flawed PCR tests, which exceeded the recommended cycle thresholds. This was, of course, denied fervently by the WHO, until they were ultimately forced to admit it was true all along.

In January 2021, The WHO issued a notice for its users regarding the use of PCR tests.[6] In it, they state, "WHO reminds IVD users that disease prevalence alters the predictive value of test results; as disease prevalence decreases, the risk of false positive increases."[7] They even went so far as to remind users that a positive result was not necessarily a diagnosis and was merely a factor to be considered when deciding on a final diagnosis.

"Most PCR assays are indicated as an aid for diagnosis, therefore, health care providers must consider any result in combination with timing of sampling, specimen type, assay specifics, clinical observations, patient history, confirmed the status of any contacts, and epidemiological informat ion."[8]

The mainstream media was quick to "fact-check" this and to claim that skeptics of the PCR test and the official COVID-19 positivity numbers in the mainstream media were wrong.[9] However, this was not the first time the efficacy of the PCR had been questioned. In February 2020, just as the fervor around the pandemic grew, outlets such as the BBC questioned whether tests were returning too many false NEGATIVES.[10] The Associated Press was not as quick to make corrections to that early and incorrect assertion. Unfortunately, this admission that the PCR tests were flawed nearly a year after the tests had been used to inflate COVID-19 numbers to justify lockdowns no longer mattered. The people who had implemented the tests had already used the inflated numbers to get what they wanted.

On July 21, 2021, the US Centers for Disease Control and Prevention (CDC) withdrew the PCR test as a valid method for detecting and identifying SARS-CoV-2 when they admitted the SARS-CoV-2 virus could not be identified apart from the influenza virus.[11] Michel Chossudovsky, in his book *The Worldwide Corona Crisis: Global Coup d'état Against Humanity,* points out, "What this CDC directive tacitly admits is that the PCR test does not effectively differentiate between 'SARS-CoV-2 and influenza viruses.' We have known this from the outset."[12]

Hindsight gives us an interesting perspective on the use of PCR tests and the narrative that emerged around them. The mainstream media would have you believe first that they were undercounting cases, then that they were counting cases on par with the number of cases, and finally, that the PCR test was flawed and should be replaced. What an interesting and convenient turn of events.

What Fauci, Birx and Vallance et al. Knew

Most readers will be acquainted with Dr. Anthony Fauci, but for the sake of context, a quote from Robert F. Kennedy's book, *The Real Anthony Fauci,* will be used to introduce him.

"Dr. Anthony Fauci spent half a century as America's reigning health commissar, ever preparing for his final role as Commander of history's biggest war against a global pandemic. Beginning in 1968, he occupied various posts at the National Institute of Allergy and Infectious Diseases (NIAID), serving as that agency's director since November 1984[13] ... His experiences surviving 50 years as the panjandrum of a key federal bureaucracy, having advised six presidents, the Pentagon, intelligence agencies, foreign governments, and the WHO, seasoned him exquisitely for a crisis that would allow him to wield power enjoyed by few rulers and no doctor in history."[14]

What Fauci, Dr. Birx, Dr. Robert Redfield, Sir Patrick Vallance (UK) and others in decision-making capacities knew is crucial. It is easy to forget the media's focus throughout 2020 and most of 2021. There was a hyperpartisan divide over the origin of the SARS-CoV-2 virus, so much so that anyone who questioned the origin of the coronavirus being zoonotic was immediately branded a MAGA-damaged Trump stooge.[15] There were also accusations of racism. Anyone who believed that SARS-CoV-2 virus came from a lab was engaging in anti-Asian hate. Many articles in the mainstream media framed the debate in terms of race. Helen Davidson, writing for *The Guardian*, is one such journalist who wrote in May 2020 that "the UN secretary-general said anti-foreigner sentiment has surged online and on the streets and highlighted the spread of antisemitic conspiracy theories and COVID-19-related anti-Muslim attacks." The article goes on to link President Trump's insistence upon the lab leak theory to anti-Asian hate.[16] While this article and many other mainstream journalists danced around the issue and used insinuation to smear opponents, some like Apoorva Mandavilli, a reporter for the New York Times, came right out and said it. She tweeted in May 2021 that the lab leak theory had "racist roots."[17]

Journalists like Robbie Soave, Glenn Greenwald, and *The National Review* pushed back against this narrative, pointing out that the so-called "wet market" theory was far more racist as it engages in Sinophobia and suggests that the global pandemic is caused by the eccentric and unsafe eating habits of the Chinese and the unsafe conditions of wet markets.[18] However, as more information came to light, some journalists revealed the likelihood that the pandemic actually came from the Wuhan Institute of Virology, where gain-of-function research was occurring. Gain-of-function research is a controversial form of genetic tampering where scientists create and engineer viruses that are more powerful than those found in nature in order to study these viruses and perhaps construct defenses against th em.[19] We now know that it is just as likely, if not more likely, that the SARS-CoV-2 coronavirus came from a lab.[20] In May 2021, some fascinating revelations started to emerge—not just about the molecular makeup of the SARS-CoV-2 virus, but about the people who were supposed to be responsible for dealing with them and potentially reacting to a global pandemic. It was revealed just how much Fauci knew about the lab leak hypothesis and when.[21] Not only that, but Fauci's efforts to suppress this information were also revealed.[22]

It would appear that despite concerns raised by Jeremy Farrar of the Wellcome Trust and Coalition for Epidemic Preparedness Innovations (CEPI)—now the WHO's Chief Scientist (how convenient)—Fauci was quick to dismiss the potential of a lab leak theory as "conspiracy" and "nonsense." Fauci actively tried to establish an early narrative by insisting upon the "proximal origins" paper led by Kristian Andersen.[23] Despite Fauci being the one to authorize research in the Wuhan Institute of Virology, and despite people in his own inner circle calling attention to the possibility of a lab leak theory, Fauci denied the possibility.

While the leaked email exchanges make it difficult to believe he did not know how likely a lab leak might be, his relationship with Dr. Ralph Baric is particularly damning. Baric is a colleague of Fauci going back almost to the 1990s, and he was known affectionately as a "coronavirus hunter" since that is what his research at Chapel Hill University centered on. In 2007, Baric's patent for his reverse genetics process, which sounds troublingly like gain of function research, was approved.[24] His goal was to make use of his research for commercial reasons, and Fauci supported him in his effort. It is now obvious why Baric was interested in the commercial applications, as there seemed a huge potential for profit. Baric, however, was not the only one who wanted to become fabulously wealthy from coronaviruses.

MODERN RNA (Moderna) is a Product of US Defense and the CIA

Moderna is a company that has long been positioned as a tool of the WEF. Going back to 2013, Moderna was named one of a handful of Global Growth Companies[25] by the WEF. The CEO of the company, Stéphane Bancel, is an alumnus of the Young Global Leaders Program.[26] The company has many connections to GAVI, the Vaccine Alliance, and the Bill and Melinda Gates Foundation, at least as far back as 2017.[27]

From its inception, Moderna has been heavily reliant on some interesting funding sources. The first is the Biomedical Advanced Research and Development Authority (BARDA), a division of US Health and Human Services.[28] BARDA is essentially a shell company for the Department of Defense (DoD), as the DoD has been using BARDA to funnel money throughout the pandemic.[29] Other major funding sources for Moderna include the Bill and Melinda Gates Foundation, which is listed as a "strategic collaborator" on their website, and the CEPI, which is a joint project of the Norwegian and Indian governments with the WEF and the Bill and Melinda Gates Foundation, and acts similarly to how BARDA acts for the DoD—to funnel money toward projects and outlets that continue the endeavors of the WEF.

Here again, we see the web of connections all leading back to the WEF with Stephan Bancal heading up Moderna, and Moderna board member Moncef Slaoui being appointed by Donald Trump to be one of the principal architects of Operation Warp Speed.[30] In this, we see the level of control the WEF has in its ability to influence and indoctrinate people in authority toward their philosophy. In the same way the WEF used various organizations as conduits for their members to have prominent roles in the UN and other supranational organizations, the pandemic provided an opportunity for people sympathetic to the WEF's goals to be put into positions of prominence in powerful governmental operations.

Perhaps this is why former Goldman Sachs analyst and eventual Prime Minister of the UK, Rishi Sunak, knew to be an early investor in Moderna through Theleme Partners.[31] Theleme Partners is a private investment partnership (hedge fund) based in London, that has nearly a billion-dollar stake in Moderna. Sunak faced questions about his involvement with the hedge fund since the beginning of the pandemic, as evidenced by a 2020 article from *The Guardian*.[32] How and why did Theleme Partners invest when Moderna had no product or revenue stream?

This is the government and the WEF picking winners and losers at an extreme level. The argument might be that this money was an investment, so the COVID-19 pandemic could be contained. They did it to save lives, one might say. Unfortunately, it would seem that the trials conducted were woefully inadequate, and that the vaccines were not as safe as originally expected, perhaps doing more damage than good. We will explore these safety issues in the next chapter.

Conclusion

As the opening months of the pandemic progressed to the first year and beyond, certain policies that had been enacted as temporary and emergency measures are still being used to this day despite questions about their efficacy. Fauci obscured the true origin of the virus and Moderna, who stood to benefit from the scenario, positioning themselves along with other pharmaceutical companies and drug manufacturers as the one and only solution.

It would seem, based on what we know now, that there was a plan put into place by the DoD, the CIA, the WEF, and the UN. This plan was to seize control of relevant agencies and develop a narrative that pointed to mRNA vaccines being the only solution to the COVID-19 problem. They ensured all information was filtered through people adhering to the plan, so that they could massage any data to fit their narrative.

Now that we have seen the spurious justifications for the actions of the people pushing these policies and mandates, we can question what, and who, was to gain. In the next chapter, we discuss how these pandemic-related policies affected individual freedom, national sovereignty, the global economy, people's health, and the choices people made. We will see how the pandemic, and the reaction to it, benefited certain parties. A timeline will emerge, and certain goals will become apparent.

Chapter 6

Pandemic or Scamdemic? Part 2

Having looked at how the pandemic narrative was framed from the very beginning, we can consider the true intentions of the global lockdowns. We were told such lockdowns were medically necessary and warranted. In many places, enforcement akin to martial law occurred. In places like Sydney[1] and Saskatchewan[2] and of course China,[3] the military was deployed to assist in compliance.

Were the Global lockdowns warranted or justified medically? Was there sufficient evidence to institute such draconian measures? In November 2022, Dr. Anthony Fauci was asked about these topics in a congressional deposition. Dr. Fauci famously obfuscated, evaded, and claimed not to remember relevant facts in his seven-hour deposition. In this deposition, he also failed to make a case for lockdown efficacy, instead pointing to China's efforts as proof that the lockdowns were necessary. Fauci discussed the advice of Clifford Lane, Fauci's deputy at the National Institute of Allergy and Infectious Disease, who claimed that China had contained the virus with draconian lockdowns. Despite China's evidence of a dictatorial leader and a tenuous relationship with data, Fauci trusted this now observably false claim.[4]

Researchers from Georgetown, the University of South Florida, and the University of New Orleans make the case compellingly that "restrictions have not been accompanied by the epistemic practices morally required for their adoption or continuation."[5] Why were authorized therapies and repurposed drugs banned with wartime-style propaganda campaigns while highly published and peer-reviewed medical professionals were silenced on social media and other forums—only some three years later, now to be given efficacy again?

Why is the global Vaccine Adverse Event Reporting System (VAERS) being ignored? Is the intelligence community driving the mRNA platform above everything else for the transhumanist 2030 agenda?

Pfizer lied in authorization documents saying the Spike-Protein stayed at the injection site; within hours, it was actually all over the body, especially in the ovaries, the heart, the liver, and spleen.[6] Why are oncologists seeing a considerable rise in rare and dormant cancers—the roles of p53, BRCA1 and BRCA2 genes etc.[7]

These and many other concerns linger as more information comes to light regarding the pandemic, the vaccine, and who knew what and when. This chapter will continue to explore the dangers of the vaccine, the dangers of the lockdown, and how this could all fit into a chilling, long-term plan.

The mRNA Vaccine

The mainstream media has made much about the safety and efficacy of the COVID-19 vaccines. Throughout the pandemic, skeptics have been ostracized, name-called, and silenced. Indeed, they were even called a danger to society.[8] However, the narrative surrounding COVID-19 vaccines has evolved. Initially, vaccines were needed to prevent the spread to others. It was a selfless act done to protect those who could not or would not get the shot. As more data came out, it was revealed the vaccines did not stop the transmission of the disease. They did not even stop the symptoms of the disease. At best, they reduced symptoms.

The CDC has redefined its stance on what the vaccines can do, from stopping transmission to preventing infection, and eventually, merely reducing symptoms. Even PolitiFact has caught on to this reality and rightfully fact-checked President Joe Biden when he claimed getting vaccinated would prevent the spread of COVID-19 to others.[9]

Seeing changes over time like this makes one wonder what the next evolution might be. While in February 2021, the Biden administration might have reached out to Twitter to silence people who questioned the efficacy of masks or how well the vaccine might prevent the spread of COVID-19,[10] some claims made today, which are seen by the mainstream as heretical right now, could well be accepted as fact in the next year or two.

One observation that has not received major media attention is that of blood clotting. It is not controversial to say that COVID-19 may cause blood clotting.[11] The spike protein present in the SARS-CoV-2 virus can sometimes trigger a clotting cascade that leads to abnormally large blood clots, some as long as a foot long.[12] What is less scientifically acknowledged is that spike proteins are produced in the body at the cellular level via the mRNA technology in the COVID-19 vaccines, which can cause the same issues as the virus itself, including abnormally large blood clots and "epithelial cell clotting cascade."[13]

Further suspicious occurrences include a study of what is called "long COVID." A study in The Lancet indicates that the more recently someone has obtained a vaccine or a booster shot, the more likely they are to experience symptoms associated with long COVID—symptoms such as fatigue, sleep issues, migraines, and other lingering effects for weeks or months after contracting the virus. It is not suggested that the vaccine causes long COVID, rather it indicates the vaccine could be weakening the body's ability to recover.[14]

Meanwhile, other illnesses are putting pressure on healthcare systems. For example, instances of respiratory syncytial virus (RSV) in infants are seven times higher than they were pre-COVID-19.[15] This surge in cases has prompted some to wonder what is causing this sudden spike in cases. One theory states that RSV is more severe in COVID-19-vaccinated children due to the vaccine destroying their hematopoietic cells.[16]

Hematopoietic cells are important intermediate cells in the cell production process, and failing to produce these cells can cause illness and the inability to fight disease and infection. In the same way the vaccine mirrors the SARS-CoV-2 virus regarding the risk of blood clots, so does the vaccine "impair the functionalities and survivability of" hematopoietic cells, akin to the way the virus does.[17]

An unlikely source of anti-vaccine sentiment has come from inside the medical industry. Throughout the pandemic, doctors and nurses at the forefront have pushed back against vaccine mandates and against getting vaccinated at all. Many healthcare workers voiced concerns, such as their natural immunity being sufficient, lack of research and safety protocols, and potential fertility issues. Other healthcare professionals objected to threats of being fired.[18] Even doctors who objected to this at the time have since spoken out about vaccine injuries they are now suffering from. One such example is Dr. Karyn Phelps, who claims she was mistreated and silenced by the Australian Parliament when she tried to tell the truth about what happened to her.[19] Mainstream outlets like NPR[20] and NBC News[21] covered protests by groups such as America's Healthcare Workers for Medical Freedom but did so dismissively.

Now, all the fears of these healthcare workers are being validated as more and more information comes out. We know the vaccine affects menstrual cycles, and we know these changes were drastically underreported.[22] There is also evidence there has been a decline in birthrates, possibly due to the vaccine. According to Mary Beth Pfeiffer, the vaccine is associated with a massive decline in births. Statistical modeling has revealed "a striking temporal correlation between the peak of the first vaccination and the decline in births in Switzerland."[23]

Given what Pfizer knew from the Phase I vaccine trials, pregnant women, who to this day are told to avoid things such as hay fever remedies, natural yogurt and blue cheese, should not have been coerced through guilt into taking a new and potentially dangerous product. Especially after some members of the medical community were being silenced for promoting the efficacy of natural immunity. In 2021, a medical study stated that "while vaccinations are highly effective at protecting against infection and severe COVID-19 disease, our review demonstrates that natural immunity in COVID-19-recovered individuals is at least equivalent to the protection afforded by complete vaccination,"[24] or as the CDC had to admit, some-times better. [25]

Is it any wonder these problems would emerge? The operation ran at "warp speed," after all. Only now are regulators asking questions and blowing whistles. Sites were left uninspected, and the process was obscured. To this day, there is nothing close to the usual regulatory process applied to vaccine manufacturing to ensure toxins and contaminants are excluded from the product. Dr. Robert Malone has pointed out many times that since pharmaceutical companies will not release a complete component list, "a regulatory agency or someone else empowered [should] test the lots coming off of the line rigorously in a controlled way with a clear chain of custody as they have always done in the past."[26] Unfortunately, the manufacturers have forbidden this.

Dr. Peter McCullough has been particularly dogged on this topic and has pointed out that the US FDA has been willfully blind to the safety of COVID-19 vaccines.[27] Drug manufacturers have been allowed to produce and manufacture their products with little to no oversight, and it may have already led to irreversible harm and catastrophic damage, not only to people who have taken the vaccine but also to the trust and faith people put in the healthcare system as a whole.

"Regulatory documents show that only nine out of 153 Pfizer trial sites were subject to FDA inspection before licensing the mRNA vaccine. Similarly, only ten out of ninety-nine Moderna trial sites and five of seventy-three remdesivir trial sites were inspected. Now, facing a backlog of site inspections, experts have criticized [sic] the FDA's oversight of clinical trials, describing it as 'grossly inadequate.'"[28]

For the truths he tried to tell, Dr. McCullough had his board certifications revoked.[29] And for all that, Dr. McCullough may be too magnanimous with his assessment that clinical trials were not conducted. New evidence suggests the trials were actually conducted, but the results were covered up. In a bombshell document dump of Pfizer vaccine data, one that Pfizer wanted hidden for fifty-five years, tens of thousands of adverse findings were discovered, including 1,200 deaths. Failed pregnancy data was conveniently dropped from the trial as well. "By February 2021, Pfizer had already received over 1,200 reports of deaths allegedly caused by the vaccine and tens of thousands of reported adverse events, including twenty-three cases of spontaneous abortions out of 270 pregnancies and over 2,000 reports of cardiac disorders."[30] It is possible these adverse events are because the SARS-CoV-2 virus has actually never even been successfully isolated and purified, as is usually a standard procedure for products such as these.[31]

Chillingly, the concerns raised by healthcare professionals throughout 2021, which were proven valid throughout 2022, may only be the beginning; there is new, correlative evidence that excess mortality is increasing in some troubling ways.[32]

The constant fear of myocarditis has never been properly discussed, and the dangers are not presented to parents of boys who are at the most significant risk of the diagnosis. The issues have been identified in several studies, one of which used data from Kaiser Permanente,[33] and alarm bells have been rung by people like Dr. Robert Malone, Dr. Vinay Prasad, and Rav Arora,[34] but there seems to be little uptake by healthcare leaders, political leaders, or the mainstream media.

A recent study highlighted on Peter McCullough's substack points out that "Nuclear translocation of spike mRNA and protein is a novel pathogenic feature of SARS-CoV-2," meaning that both the SARS-CoV-2 virus and the COVID-19 vaccine itself could reduce the body's ability to fight cancer cell creation.[35]

This study aligns with what some oncologists are saying about the effect of booster shots on patients who have cancer.[36] Multiple signs point to certain cancers being exacerbated by both the COVID-19 vaccine and the SARS-CoV-2 virus, although it is not only oncologists noticing the phenomenon.

Recently, a Belgian immunologist named Dr. Michel Goldman went public with the news his lymphoma was worsening, possibly due to having the Pfizer vaccine. Even after the diagnosis, he struggled with whether or not to reveal this publicly, as he felt beholden to a system that kept things like this quiet. In the past, he had even suggested that discussing side effects was a bad idea, since they could use such issues as an argument against vaccination. Being confronted with his own vaccine injury, he begrudgingly changed his mind.[37]

It is hard to fault Dr. Goldman's reluctance to speak out when one considers the story of Dr. Daniel Nagase and Dr. Melvin Bruchet. Dr. Nagase was fired for utilizing the medically useful, but controversial, ivermectin as a treatment for COVID-19 (which, incidentally, might be a treatment for cancer),[38] while Bruchet was arrested for discussing the drastic increase of stillbirths in a Vancouver hospital. The two doctors have since been the victims of smear campaigns from the likes of Vancouver Coastal Health, a health service agency that dominates the West Coast of Canada. The mainstream media, such as Canadian Broadcasting Corporation, CTV, and Global News, have joined in the smear campaign as well.[39] It is no wonder more healthcare professionals do not come forward.

The increase in these maladies may be linked to Graphene Oxide, which Spanish researchers may have located in Pfizer vials. Graphene oxide has led to apoptosis or programmed cell death.[40]

When the UK's regulatory agency, Medicines and Healthcare products Regulatory Agency (MHRA), was pressed about this, the group pushed back and claimed Pfizer's right to trade secrets trumped the public's right to safety, calling requests for information about what is in the vaccine "exempt from release under Section 41 (information provided in confidence) and Section 43 (commercial interests) of the Freedom of Information (FOI) Act." The MHRA stated in the same missive that they "have considered the public interest and cannot see any public interest argument that outweighs the commercial harm in releasing information."[41] Why even have regulatory agencies when they lack the will to investigate claims of malfeasance?

As if there needed to be any further evidence of these issues, doctors are now looking for blood that has not been tainted by vaccines.[42] Will this be the new normal?

The Case for Regulation

In January 2022, researchers at Stanford University published a paper entitled "Immune Imprinting, Breadth of Variant Recognition, and Germinal Center Response in Human SARS-CoV-2 Infection and Vaccination." This study, according to the aforementioned researcher Dr. Robert Malone, asks questions that the FDA did not ask when the vaccines were being approved, such as "How long is the RNA there? How long is the protein, spike protein, being made? How much spike protein is being made?" Dr. Malone makes the case that these are "Fundamental questions that should have been known at the very beginning." Malone explains that the FDA did not ask these questions because the intelligence community and the White House did not want their endeavor to be slowed down. To expedite the process, the FDA "did a little hand waving," as Malone calls it, and classified the products as mRNA vaccines rather than what they really are, which is gene therapy. Classifying the product as a vaccine ensures that it will be subjected to a safety checklist that differs significantly from a gene therapy checklist. They sped the process up according to the dictates of Operation Warp Speed to ensure the product would be approved.

Malone also questions the efficacy of the vaccine against natural immunity. To question this is to question what is now a multibillion-dollar endeavor. Malone's opinion could be considered controversial in that vaccine manufacturers such as Pfizer and Moderna could have a vested interest in silencing dissenters, or disproving counter theories in whatever way they can.

Malone makes a point of noting the difference between "payload" and "platform." The mRNA platform technology is the ability of the product to deliver customized genetic information to treat a patient's symptoms. The mRNA platform includes everything necessary to manufacture and deliver the RNA so that customizable medicine can treat individuals, or mass vaccination efforts can be quickly mobilized when new pathogens emerge because the mRNA platform infrastructure is in place.

The "payload" is an informal term used by virologists for the protein that is delivered. The spike protein and the RNA coding of the spike protein are the payloads of the COVID-19 vaccine. How it is packaged, assembled, manufactured, tested, et cetera, is the platform. This is the key to understanding the long-term goals for mRNA technology and for understanding how the state will use it in the future.[43]

How the CIA and DoD Were Utilized to Facilitate the Vaccine Rollout

In April 2021, there was a WHO conference where Dr. Margaret Liu of Merck, among others, met with regulatory agencies from around the world and agreed to "circumvent normal preclinical and clinical testing." The agencies could do this because they were approving the platform rather than the payload. This was the bait and switch they used at the highest levels of decision-making to circumvent individual choice, liberty, and consent.

Dr. Robert Malone claims this is all in an effort to utilize mRNA technologies with the COVID-19 pandemic and in future crises.

"The truth is that DARPA [Defense Advanced Research Projects Agency], which is the operational development arm, basically the CIA, fell in love with the RNA technology over a decade ago. They decided to capitalize on it and force it into the market space. For instance, they're the ones that have capitalized through In-Q-Tel, their investment arm, the new RNA manufacturing facilities up in Canada. This is a CIA program. There's no ambiguity here. I'm not telling state secrets... DARPA funded and basically built Moderna. They're continuing to push all this. They're pushing it through the government. What you're seeing is the power of the intelligence community and the new bio-defense industrial complex that's developed since the anthrax attacks, and it really goes beyond that in being able to push their agenda through the government."[44]

In retrospect, much of the justification used for mandates has come under fire. Key decision-makers, such as Deborah Birx, have even since admitted that certain "science-based" measures were essentially made up. For example, Birx admitted in her memoirs that some of the mitigation measures were made up and arbitrary. Using the initial recommendations for the size of gatherings as an example, Birx discusses her desire for it to be capped at ten, while the CDC offered the upper limit of fifty. "I had settled on ten knowing that even that was too many, but I figured that ten would at least be palatable for most Americans..."[45] She is critical of Marc Short from Mike Pence's Vice President's office who "asked if there was a scientific basis for fifty versus ten." That the Republican political advisor to Mike Pence—a man who believes creationism should be taught in schools—had to ask Dr. Birx for scientific underpinnings for her recommendations reveals just how arbitrary they really were. Birx also admitted to manipulating data in reports to the vice president's office to allow for more stringent mitigation measures, admitted to the possibility that the SARS-CoV-2 virus came from a lab (contradicting early statements she had made), and amended her stance on the virus' ability to prevent infection.[46] Point by point, the narrative constructed by this high-ranking official has been undone. Dr. Birx is now openly admitting information that, at the time, would have gotten her removed from the public squares of Twitter and Facebook in mid-2020.

We can see now that manipulating the data to hand over more power to the Governors is part and parcel of the UN's efforts to circumvent sovereignty. Birx's manipulation of the data is the blueprint for obtaining control.

The Dangers of the Lockdowns

There was skepticism about the efficacy of a lockdown and the economic damage that a circuit-breaker lockdown could do from the beginning.[47]

Debates about Sweden's policies have raged and caused Twitter debates for years.[48] The "Great Lockdown" led to global contractions of economies and what the IMF called the "Worst Economic Downturn Since the Great Depression."[49]

There are many harms caused by lockdowns that are not easily quantifiable. Some issues caused because of lockdowns include an increase in drug and alcohol use, an increase in relapses amongst those suffering from addiction, an increase in cases of suicide, lack of access to treatment for those who have cancer and cardiovascular diseases, a loss of basic social skills for children, an increase in domestic violence, an increase in homelessness, and pollution from single-use plastic and PPE increased. Also, personal finances took a major hit because of the lockdowns, with bankruptcy, unemployment, and personal debt all increasing as a result.[50]

But perhaps these things were intentional. Is it possible the lockdowns were orchestrated to trash the economy, create chaos and fear in citizens across the globe, hand power to globalist monopolies, and then lay the groundwork for various measures such as CBDCs, vaccine passports, and social media reeducation camps? If you look at how the WEF, the WHO, and the UN acted, you might fight your answer.

Linking the WHO, the WEF and the UN with COVID-19 Compliance

The idea of a pandemic treaty is presented as a somewhat noncontroversial idea.[51] Particularly in the shadow of all the fear cultivated throughout 2020 and 2021, there is widespread acceptance, if not support, of the idea of pooling international resources to recruit health personnel, prepare for influenza outbreaks, and educate the public on health concerns. However, when member nations push back, it becomes apparent that a pandemic treaty is about more than distributing pamphlets and sharing resources. It is about dictating policy, sidestepping sovereignty, and maintaining control.

The proposal of the WHO to incorporate 194 member nations into a pandemic treaty presents the possibility of creating a health-orientated "back door" to a new world order. The WHO already wields tremendous power. "The WHO has the constitutional power to create treaty law and nonbinding instruments and recommendations."[52] A pandemic treaty would expand that power immensely.

If there is any doubt that the attempts to cope with the COVID-19 pandemic are not focused on helping or treating patients, one need look no further than the person appointed to be Biden's COVID-19 czar, Dr. Ashish Jha. He came to his position by systematically waging a propaganda campaign against doctors who were treating COVID-19 patients and developing therapy protocols from their first-hand experiences. Dr. Ashish Jha was hired, it seems, more for his political ideology, rhetorical skills, and willingness to adhere to the official narrative rather than his experience treating COVID-19, as it was revealed during a contentious Senate hearing that he had never treated a COVID-19 patient.[53]

So often, these are the people who end up in positions of power—not the people who are most qualified, but people who are willing to do the bidding of their superiors.

Conclusion

This all leads to why some of these baffling decisions were made. Dr. Robert Malone has his theories. He has gone on a speaking tour trying to highlight the work of Dr. Mattias Desmet, an expert in mass hypnosis and what might be called "the madness of crowds." Dr. Mattias Desmet is a psychologist and a statistician at the University of Ghent in Belgium. He calls the phenomena we are seeing in response to mass COVID-19 vaccine compliance "Mass Formation Psychosis."[54]

This form of temporary psychosis can be cultivated by severing the bonds of social connectedness (through "short-term" lockdowns, for example), ratcheting up anxiety (through inflated infection and mortality numbers), and then offering a single solution that encourages those subjected to these maneuvers to become hostile to alternate thoughts.

The mass formation hypothesis, combined with the opacity of vaccine information, becomes potentially dire when the long-term likely goals are considered. What is that long-term goal? Certainly, a UN-orchestrated, one-world government is one outcome. Klaus Schwab and the WEF's Great Reset is another potential goal of the people who have perpetrated these policies. One potential outcome is even more dire than these possibilities. This potential outcome can be found on the Deagel website. Deagel is a news site that provides users with information about international military aviation and advanced technologies. It is an independent organization, but it has been known to have links to some intelligence organizations like Stratfor as well as the UN and the White House. With these bona fides, it is troubling to find that in 2014, the website made some dire predictions for the time period of 2015-2025. Their predictions included upwards of a twenty-five to eighty percent drop in population in many western nations. Their justification for this predictive modeling is a changing economic paradigm.

"Historically, a change in the economic paradigm has resulted in a death toll that is rarely highlighted by mainstream historians. When the transition from rural areas to large cities happened in Europe, many people unable to accept the new paradigm killed themselves. They killed themselves by a psychological factor. This is not mainstream, but it is true. A new crisis joins old, well-known patterns with new ones."[55]

Was their model correct? Was it merely a thought experiment, a hoax, or does this organization with access to national intelligence agencies and vast amounts of data know something most people do not? Only time will tell, but this predictive model fits in with the contours of the Great Reset in some troubling ways.

It is an age-old question: was it malevolence or incompetence? There is evidence for both cases. On the one hand, government bureaucracies often attach themselves to one simple idea, and unquestioning bureaucrats carry out orders and maintain fidelity and adherence to the official story without considering the truth. This is not a new occurrence. They persecuted Copernicus and Plato for their beliefs, and we now consider their previously considered heretical beliefs to be commonplace and easy to accept. What are today's controversies that will be tomorrow's truth?

Then again, when all the information is lined up, and the players' associations and actions are revealed, the other narrative emerges. One where everything from the groundwork to the catastrophic event to the solution were all orchestrated by a relatively small group of people, all of whom had a long-term ulterior motive. With the fog of the pandemic finally lifting from most people's eyes, there are lessons learned and, hopefully, lessons that can be applied to the next mass formation event. Lori Weintz of the Brownstone Institute offers wise words on this subject when she says, "A repeat of the medical tyranny we were subjected to during the pandemic, and the fulfillment of a vision of a 'digital transformation of the world,' will only happen if we comply."[56]

This will be important to keep in mind in the next chapter when we discuss climate change and the way it is being utilized by the same people who made use of the global pandemic to attain their own ends.

Chapter 7

It's the sUN Driving the Climate, Not hUmaNs

The Intergovernmental Panel on Climate Change (IPCC) has established the narrative regarding climate change.[1] Most major news organizations, cultural outlets, global world leaders, and the UN agree with the IPCC's findings on climate change.[2] These groups describe climate change as a human-created problem caused by the burning of fossil fuels, which release carbon into the air. The consequences of this change in climate can include droughts, water scarcity, forest fires, and the melting of the polar ice caps, thus leading to flooding and rising sea levels. Sea levels might rise so high that some coastal cities will end up under water.[3]

A common talking point amongst the mainstream media is that 99 percent of the relevant scientists agree climate change is real, and that it is manmade. They would have you believe, the skepticism you see comes from a tiny minority. Anyone who pushes back against the majority's narrative, risks the accusation of being an agent of the oil companies, having a political agenda, or just being plain wrong. But is this true? Are there perhaps any other reasons climate change may be pushed to the forefront of people's consciousness? What are the unintended consequences of climate change? Is there a narrative surrounding climate change that is being suppressed? This chapter explores these questions and considers how the climate change narrative may be used to manipulate the public into obedience.

Controlling the Data Is Controlling the Argument

A Fairleigh Dickinson University poll reveals a more nuanced representation of the "consensus" opinion of climate change. The data show that up to forty-one percent of scientists, including climatologists and members of the American Meteorology Society, think that the climate will not get significantly worse in the near future, with some even going so far as to say that the climate will improve.[4] This is a far cry from what most cable news networks would lead you to believe when they make the broad and context-lacking statement that ninety-nine percent of climate scientists agree. Reframing the data in this way allows us to see an effort to characterize the debate surrounding climate change. However, reframing data so it seems to say something that it does not, is not the only way the conversation is being cajoled.

Another similar case of selection bias is that of the UK's Royal Air Force (RAF) meteorological data. They made much of the July 19, 2022, UK high of 40.3°C (104.5 degrees Fahrenheit) recorded at RAF Coningsby.[5] This would certainly be notable, if true, but it makes one wonder why other data, like the record low temperature of -45.2 degrees Celsius (-49 degrees Fahrenheit) at the South Pole in the same year[6] is not as widely discussed and reported upon.

Not only was the heat spike countered by a cold spike, but the truth of the sudden heat spike was later called into question, as solar radiation or a jet exhaust potentially caused it.[7] Even if the data were accurate, this obscuring of such data calls into question the overall narrative. Time and time again, we see cracks in the narrative and holes in the story. Eventually, it should prompt one to wonder why it is so important for mainstream media, academia, governments, and global intergovernmental collabora-tives to insist upon favoring some data whilst burying other data.

According to Professor Richard Muller, an emeritus professor of physics at the University of California, the science has been settled and skepticism is no longer valid. He has been very vocal about his views on how the temperature has increased by more than a degree centigrade since 1950 and is continuing to warm. His organization, the Berkeley Earth Surface Temperatures (BEST) project, has made concerted efforts to warn about the potential for flooding, unforeseen weather events, and a possible global species collapse. BEST released findings to the public in October 2011 and was met with a deluge of media coverage from outlets such as the BBC,[8] the *Economist*,[9] and *Science Daily*.[10] There was very little critique of BEST's findings, with most media coverage seeming to take the data as complete, moving straight on to discussions about how to solve the looming climate catastrophe. However, some people did speak out. One such person said, "There is no scientific basis for saying that warming hasn't stopped." This person was not a cable news pundit nor a member of the general public. She was a woman named Professor Judith Curry, and she has her own impressive CV, including that of a distinguished climate researcher with over thirty years of experience in the field. She is also listed as a co-author of Muller's paper, as she is a member of the BEST project. She pointed out that there was something untruthful about Professor Muller's statement. Her main concern was about the integrity of the data. "To say that there is [warming] detracts from the credibility of the data, which is very unfo rtunate."[11] Curry was able to show that rates had actually declined for the decade preceding the release of the findings. While she still had concerns about climate change, she worried Muller's instinct to release incomplete data would hurt their case in the long run. She was right. For more than a decade, people have defended Muller and the BEST project, but the fact remains, he failed to release all the relevant data, which has given climate skeptics the justification to continue questioning the prominent narrative.

The BEST incident recalls the "Climategate" scandal of 2009, where Professor Phil Jones, who headed up the Climatic Research Unit (CRU) at the University of East Anglia (UEA) in the UK, was found to have suppressed data that contradicted certain claims his research had made. Even articles from mainstream news sources trying to dismiss claims of wrongdoing are forced to admit that such attempts to cover up information, hide data, and obfuscate the truth "call into question the probity of some climate change science."[12]

An article in *Forbes* responding to what they called 2011's "Climategate 2.0," yet another shocking and anonymous leak of over 5,000 emails, summed up all these disputes and scandals nicely:

1. Prominent scientists central to the global warming debate are taking measures to conceal rather than disseminate underlying data and discussions.

2. These scientists view global warming as a political "cause" rather than a balanced scientific inquiry.

3. Many of these scientists frankly admit to each other that much of the science is weak and dependent on deliberate manipulation of facts and data.[13]

It is this kind of manipulation and obfuscation that causes skeptics to question the prevalent narrative, and these incidents are far from the only examples. It also prompts many to ask, what is there to gain from raising alarm bells about climate science and who will benefit?

Suppressing data gathered from the past is one thing. The other major issue with much of the climate science prominent in the mainstream is that it is based on computer models and predictions for what might happen to ice caps and weather patterns in the future, which is a notoriously unreliable endeavor. Such models are so unreliable, they caused Greg Chapman, a former computer modeler with a Ph.D. in Physics, to claim that "any model will be a poor predictor of the future."[14]

So, if the datasets from the past are manipulated, and the models about the future are unreliable, how is there such consensus about the climate?

Natural Climate Variability

The mainstream mantra insists that "climate change is real, and it is caused by people."[15] While the existence of climate change has been called into doubt by climate scientists' reluctance to share their data, it follows logically that the second half of that claim may also be questionable.

It is not controversial to say the Earth's natural tendency is toward drastic climatological shifts. The planet has gone through various periods of being inordinately hot and exceedingly cold. Many of these periods of extreme temperatures in either direction occurred before humans even had a chance to make an impact on the globe. What is slightly more controversial is the statement that many non-anthropic factors could also be the reason for such fluctuations occurring. For instance, volcanic sulfur, orbital wobbles, and, of course, solar cycles. Despite how unpopular this opinion might be, it is verifiably true.[16]

Solar cycles, in particular, have an impact on Earth's climate to this day.[17] These eleven-year cycles occur because of magnetic pole shifts, and they can be tumultuous or mild. Indeed, tumultuous solar cycles throughout the end of the 20th century correspond to increased global temperatures, while a less turbulent sun cycle around 2014 resulted in more stable global temperatures.[18] Solar cycles are often ignored when it comes to discussion of climate change, in favor of human-created sources like increased use of fossil fuels, deforestation, and methane gas excreted by livestock;[19] but this factor is an important one, one which should not be ignored. Even if the first half of the statement "climate change is real..." proves to be true, it is still incumbent upon the claimants to prove the second half, "...and caused by people," true as well.

What Is Their Solution to Climate Change?

While climate change believers are in agreement regarding the existence of anthropogenic climate change, there is a significant amount of debate and controversy, even among this homogenous group, about whether or not proposed mitigation strategies will work.

Some advocate for the increased use of renewable energy, such as wind and solar power, to facilitate the reduction of greenhouse gas emissions, but the cost of making this switch is so prohibitively expensive and such a strain on infrastructure, that even advocates at the highest levels know it is untenable. Renewable energy sources are so unreliable that they bring with them a significant increase in the cost of electricity.[20] Also, they bring with them a host of unforeseen consequences, for example, the unintended impact of windmills on bird populations.[21] Other widely championed effort of climate believers are reforestation and energy conserving technologies in cars and factories. Reforestation is a proactive effort to utilize natural carbon dioxide processes to reduce carbon; however, these efforts are likely to fail, because the growing population needs land for housing instead of forests.[22] Energy conserving technologies are sometimes cumbersome and expensive to use as they actually require more time, energy, and money to operate.

While all of these efforts come with alleged mitigations to the purported climate issues, it is telling that there is not more political will to implement them on a wide scale. It is almost as if the people proposing these various solutions have no interest in actually following through with their implementation.

Some have made the case for geoengineering, which has proven to be controversial. Making changes to the environment, such as cloud seeding to block out UV rays, has gone against the orthodoxy of forcing complicity and submission to punitive global regimes. This reveals something about the debate. Assuming climate change is occurring and needs to be addressed, why are certain approaches being given such preferential treatment over others? One of the biggest developments in climate science of the past ten years is the development of geoengineering technologies.[23] Many activists are worried that carbon dioxide removal technologies will detract from climate change mitigation efforts, that they will cost too much, or that nations will see them as a license to keep polluting.[24]

It is almost as if solving the climate change problem is not the goal. In the same way a cult leader continuously warns of the end of the world, only to announce on doomsday that they had been miraculously saved by prayer, the dire warnings and predictions of people like Al Gore have failed to materialize, and the performative efforts of planting trees and raising taxes on companies that cause pollution are pointed to as reasons for the reprieve.[25] This kind of environmental alarmism has been going on since at least the 1970s when they announced the first Earth Day.[26]

The real goal seems to be universal submission, not international agreements like the Paris Climate Agreement and the Kyoto accords. These dictatorial efforts lorded over by organizations such as the UN are systems of control that dictate who can use which resources and when. These systems come with punitive tools and restrictive austerity measures. This suggests the real reason for climate change alarmism and might explain why the solutions that could actually work are not being implemented.

Consequences of Climate Policies

Climate change is beginning to be a catch-all excuse for many of the ills of society. For example, recently, the UK Health Security Agency (UKHSA) Chief Jenny Harries blamed excess deaths in the UK on climate change. She ignored the possibility that warmer weather might cause milder winters and thus fewer deaths and chose instead to focus on the idea that climate change was responsible for increased deaths in the summer, along with possibly causing food shortages and malaria outbreaks.[27] This is part of a larger trend of pointing to climate change as a reason for many problems. According to the WEF, for example, climate change could be the reason behind everything from lightning strikes to plane crashes to the quality of your coffee and wine.[28]

New and unexpected victims of these global policies are being revealed. One such unintended consequence is the risk now facing the Zambezi

Watercourse in southern Africa. Greenhouse gas reduction techniques threaten to dry out the Zambezi Watercourse, which sustains many local communities. Implementing these mitigation policies will risk habitat collapse in the area and possibly disperse entire communities.[29]

While some consequences of climate change policy are unintended, others are very much intended. A 2019 survey of the Association for Financial Inclusion survey found that over seventy-five percent of member nations already included climate change and financial inclusion in their national financial sector strategies. One of these strategies is mobile money. Mobile money is a strategy that purports to facilitate cash transfers to marginalized populations after disasters. The strategy is a technological solution for displaced communities, and it is supposed to allow a conduit of resources to those in need after a disaster. However, critics have pointed out that this strategy, already used by so many countries, could merely be a justification for seizing control of the money supply. Global System for Mobile Communications (GSMA), which professes to be a global organization for unifying mobile ecosystems, tips its hand with its own marketing of the idea.

"There is an opportunity to strengthen global efforts to tackle climate change by leveraging existing business models that are designed to reach the marginalized [sic] and underserved. Seizing the power of mobile money for climate action calls for an increased understanding that successful solutions to drive financial inclusion can be refined and strengthened to combat climate change and its impact."[30]

When tech organizations champion the "leveraging" of business models and advocate for "seizing the power of mobile money," they are revealing their desire to dictate how money can be spent. This kind of language is not far from Chinese-style social credit scoring. The only difference is that this is on a global scale, and it uses climate change and net-zero policies as a justification for Marxism.[31]

Conclusion

The final maneuver of the climate change narrative is to turn it into a secular religion. Just ask Ivar Giaever, a Nobel Prize winner in physics, who has been highly critical of the rhetoric surrounding climate science.[32] Giaever is one of many respected scientists who has questions about global warming. A consortium of over 200 scientists claimed the UN-sponsored climate change science and associated mantras are a hoax. Yet the mainstream media silenced them and, given the Club of Rome's climate vector admissions, we might know why. The climate was carefully chosen as a "universal" problem to which elites could manipulate the data and force through their science; detractors are easily labeled as nut jobs and pro-oil shills.

Politicians and climate propagandists will frame the debate in terms of good and evil and reward those who adopt the "good" point of view while shaming those with a dissenting skeptical view. It also flatters the believer, suggesting to them that the decisions they make, down to what kind of car they drive, matter so much to the fate of the globe and human existence. Car commercials have nothing on the IPCC and their propaganda machine. If this does not work, there are always fear tactics, such as the threats of "zombie" viruses returning from the permafrost,[33] "super crabs,"[34] and gravity shifts.[35]

This makes it easy for people who do not understand the complexity of the debate. All they need to do is choose the side of the angels and fret no more. This allows the climate to be used as a justification for reclaiming private land, creating new taxes, banning citizens from waterways and the countryside, and ostracizing anyone who questions the accepted narrative.

Chapter 8

You WILL Eat the Bugs

In 2016, the WEF released a video on Facebook outlining eight predictions for 2030. The one minute and thirty-three-second video, with a thoughtful and meditative song playing in the background, lists eight predictions over sometimes aspirational, sometimes chilling, pictures. The video can still be found, but the text is reproduced below.

8 predictions for the world in 2030

Based on the input of members of the WEF's Global Future Councils

1. You'll own nothing And you'll be happy

Whatever you want you'll rent And it'll be delivered by drone

2. The US won't be the world's leading superpower

A handful of countries will dominate

3. You won't die waiting for an organ donor

We won't transplant organs

We'll print new ones instead

4. You'll eat much less meat

An occasional treat, not a staple

For the good of the environment and our health

5. A billion people will be displaced by climate change

We'll have to do a better job at welcoming and integrating refugees

6. Polluters will have to pay to emit carbon dioxide

There will be a global price on carbon

This will help make fossil fuels history

7. You could be preparing to go to Mars

Scientists will have worked out how to keep you healthy in space

The story of a journey to find alien life?

8. Western values will have been tested to the breaking point

Checks and balances that underpin our democracies must not be forgotten[1]

The video may seem baffling even on a grammatical level. The capitalization and punctuation decisions alone are curious. It has eight recommendations and only one period and one question mark. It claims to be making predictions, but it also vacillates between guessing at technological advancements and seemingly making ominous commands, perhaps even threats. The video seems to belie some underlying assumptions the WEF is making about the world's perception of certain issues.

This chapter will analyze these predictions and discuss how they fit into the WEF's agenda. It will also look at how the agenda of the WEF (along with the UN's and the Council on Foreign Relations' (CFR)) will soon be, or are already being, implemented.

Protein

We are already beginning to see the implementation of the WEF and the UN's protocols. These principles are being positioned in our culture using propaganda campaigns, with radical ideas being discussed in an attempt to normalize them. In July 2021, the WEF posted an article to their website pertaining to food security.[2]

This was not the first time this idea was presented by the WEF, as articles about the topic appeared in 2018[3] and even earlier, in a 2013 report made available to the public called "Sustainable Consumption: Stakeholder Perspectives." In the 2013 report, they stated that, "In some other cultures, insects actually serve as food. Bringing edible insects such as leafhoppers or mealworm beetle larvae onto our menus would not only supply the necessary amount of protein but also can provide jobs and income to rural producers."[4] This passage is referring to a 2008 report commissioned by none other than the UN.[5]

According to the WEF, because of the steadily increasing population and the decrease in land suitable for livestock and agriculture,[6] alternatives must be considered. This, like many of their claims, seems logical and fits into their stated mission of sustainability. Their solution, however, is for insects to become a larger and larger source of protein. This solution has been implemented and utilized across the globe for many years and now the UN aims to make it commonplace in the West.

Propagandists in the mainstream media began embracing this idea as well. Outlets like *Time*,[7] the *Washington Post*,[8] the *Guardian*,[9] and Cambridge University[10] have published articles advocating the normalization of eating insects. This is important because even as these articles receive pushback in the short term, in the long term they will more than likely, albeit slowly, become accepted. This is just one of the many ways propaganda is used to set social trends.

The first glaring problem with this policy suggestion is the hypocrisy inherent in the pronouncement. The ostensible reason for replacing animal meat with insects as a protein source is to reduce the carbon footprint and reduce the impact on climate that the cattle, poultry, and meat industries have on the environment. The problem with that is the lavish behavior of the elites who make up the WEF and UN has not gone unnoticed. The elite make up more than half of all carbon emissions, yet they strive to make the rest of the world shoulder the burden of reducing carbon emissions.[11]

While rock stars,[12] actors,[13] and even some world leaders[14] attempt to reduce their carbon footprint (regardless of how hypocritical these efforts might be),[15] these arbiters of what is right and acceptable cannot be bothered to take the same measures. They travel on their corporate jets[16] and eat the finest meals, while their literature encourages the masses to eat insects and use the bike lane.

Meanwhile, it has been discovered that chitin (in insect exoskeletons) is a potential allergy-promoting pathogen-associated molecular pattern (PAMP). In a paper published by *The Clinical Review of Allergy & Immunology*, a study found that "mammalians themselves do not synthesize chitin and thus it is considered as a potential target for recognition by the mammalian immune system."[17] This means that consuming chitin, particularly at as large a rate as the WEF might suggest, could cause severe immune and allergic responses in individuals, and such a response could be widespread among people who eat significant amounts of chitin. This, of course, leaves open the potential for new chitin-countering pharmaceutical products to be marketed and adopted widely.

Austerity as a Route to CBDCs and Universal Basic Income

Control of the food source is not the only hypocrisy and is far from the only austerity or program of control the WEF is trying to get governments to implement. As is typically the case, these efforts to strip citizens of their autonomy are disguised as efforts to protect them from some nefarious actor, or prevent the spread of terrorism, corruption, or disease. In the end, law-abiding citizens are often the only ones who have their rights curtailed.

Many of the WEF's predictions (the fifth, sixth, and to some degree, the seventh) have to do with climate change and the response to climate change. These entries are beginning to outline how climate change will be used as a justification for many new edicts. Here, the pronouns used are very interesting. First of all, the claim in prediction five is that "We'll have to do a better job at welcoming... refugees" is an interesting choice of words. Who is the "we" of this statement? The WEF has put this video together. Are they talking about themselves? Or perhaps they have elected themselves to speak on our behalf? But who is "us?" Anyone who sees the video? Only the countries espousing the "Western values" they mention later in the video? When they say "we," who do they mean? Do they mean the people of a nation? Is this "prediction" actually a command to adjust the immigration policy of sovereign nations? This is a revelation that the WEF believes they speak on behalf of all countries.

In the very next section, there is a reference to "polluters." Who are these polluters? It does not say that the owners of powerful companies will have to pay to emit carbon dioxide. It just says polluters. This could mean industries, or it could mean individuals. It could mean that anyone who emits a single gram of carbon could be fined, taxed, or charged.

It has been said that "Public finance is politics hidden in accounting co lumns."[18] This has been apparent in the British local state over the past decade. Austerity measures, put in place to achieve some larger goal, like climate change or debt reduction, often hurt the economically disenfranchised disproportionately. Local governments are forced to carry the financial burden of such measures. These austerity measures instituted at the local level are "part of a longer-term political project to reshape and redefine the welfare state at a national and local level..."[19] This should be chilling to anyone who is paying attention to the larger pattern of control instituted by international organizations but implemented by local governments.

These cuts open up governments and the populace to new solutions. These solutions include, but are not limited to, Universal Basic Income (UBI) and CBDCs. Whether these were the long-term goals of the WEF and the UN remains to be seen, but it certainly seems to fit with their long-term plans.

Job Guarantee and UBI

Modern Monetary Theory (MMT) and its proponents lay out a case for UBI. They claim that money is no longer what it once was. It represents something new in this 21st century. Money is a measure of natural resources, machine labor, human labor, knowledge, time, skill, and several other factors that all go into creating goods and services and innovating. Money, being a human construct, can be manipulated and thus, many proponents of MMT are also proponents of UBI.[20]

UBI came to prominence in the late 20th century, with even Martin Luther King at one point voicing interest in the potential for egalitarianism in the philosophy.[21] Modern proponents, who sometimes call UBI by names such as "Job Guarantee" or "Employer of Last Resort," are starting to advocate for it as a countermeasure to modern unemployment issues and increased automation.[22]

The real problem with UBI comes down to two issues. First, it is being used as a bait and switch for getting rid of what conservatives in the US derisively call "entitlement programs."[23] The programs that benefit the most economically vulnerable, like housing and food vouchers, will be cut and redistributed as UBI, much to the delight of organizations like the Adam Smith Institute.

Second, the other major question that must be asked of those who would carry out the implementation of UBI is, who decides the dollar amount? UBI is based on using MMT to determine the values of available resources and to attribute a dollar value accordingly. This is a significant amount of power, as someone with the power to manipulate value can wipe out entire industries with the stroke of a key, can devalue fortunes overnight, and redirect public policy by overvaluing certain jobs, resources, and commodities. This is an enormous amount of power, and whomever wields it will determine the direction in which society marches, although it is nothing compared to how the UBIs will be distributed.

Digital Currencies

One agency that the media does not give as much attention to as it should is the Bank for International Settlements (BIS). This organization claims that its mission is "to support central banks' pursuit of monetary and financial stability through international cooperation, and to act as a bank for central banks."[24] The BIS present itself as a means by which developing countries can mobilize funds for education and the reduction of poverty. In reality, BIS is a global banking organization working alongside The World Bank and the IMF to implement monetary strategies, which aim to force compliance among developing and impoverished nations.[25] But their reach is not limited to the developing world. The BIS has plans for wealthy nations as well, and those plans include CBDC.

According to Agustín Carstens, General Manager of the BIS, the problem with currency is that central banks cannot track it.

"We don't know who's using a 100-dollar bill today, and we don't know who's using a 1,000-peso bill today. The key difference with the CBDC is the central bank will have absolute control over the rules and regulations that will determine the use of that expression of central bank liability, and also we will have the technology to enforce that."[26]

Since 2020, there has been a rush to delegitimize cryptocurrencies and offer in their stead CBDCs with over 100 countries exploring the currency.[27]

Now, first world nations like the US[28] and the UK[29] are scrambling to create these digital currencies to control the money supply, transactions, and individual wealth in ways they never have before.

Individual Liberty

The global COVID-19 pandemic, not unlike climate change, has given the state unprecedented levels of power over individuals, allowing them to peel back hitherto inalienable and unassailable rights. While early in the pandemic a vaccine passport was unthinkable, recent developments have made them all but inevitable.[30] Travel between nations that used to be easy, like Japan and the US, are now cumbersome and complicated due to the difficulty in navigating the vaccination policies of various nations.[31] At least under these policies, citizens of these countries still have the choice to choose to be vaccinated or unvaccinated. That may soon be a thing of the past as well.

Bioethicists have taken on the role of moral arbiters of truth and have even gone so far as to recommend the coercive practice of withholding medical treatment to the unvaccinated, and discuss the use of psychoactive "morality pills" in a bid to end vaccine hesitancy.[32] And if all that fails, what better way to circumvent personal liberty and remove individual choice than to dose people secretly with whatever vaccine the elites deem necessary? A $500,000 grant from the National Science Foundation made it possible for researchers to develop mRNA vaccines that grow in spinach and lettuce plants.[33] What they don't mention is how easy it will be to get people to take it when they don't know they are taking it.

It is easy for people who consider themselves bioethicists to come to these positions when they think only in terms of inoculation, and they tell each other they are the cure for what ails society.[34] Once you think you have the moral high ground, you are capable of all kinds of atrocities.[35]

Traveling to other countries won't be the only place citizens suffer restricted access. Soon, even their own countryside will be off limits, as the seventeen UN Sustainable Development Goal mandates prevent people from going into certain places due to COVID-19-related "rewilding efforts."[36] This effort falls at the intersection of COVID-19 policy and climate policy.

The realm of vaccinations is not the only place where government overreach is occurring regularly. The policy of Net-Zero is having an enormous impact on industries as diverse as the oil industry, car manufacturing, and retail outlets. In the UK, the government plans to end the sale of new petrol and diesel cars by 2030[37] and instead, transition to toward the sole use of electric vehicles.[38] Is this because it is the only way to save the species from global collapse? Perhaps. Or perhaps it is to maintain control over the industry and help usher in Klaus Schwab's 4IR.[39]

From Global to Local: the International Council for Local Environmental Initiatives

The eighth entry in the WEF's infamous video claims, "Western values will have been tested to the breaking point" and warns, "Checks and balances that underpin our democracies must not be forgotten." This commitment to democracy is surprising given the organization is not an amalgam of Western nations, but, by the group's own literature, "outstanding firms from around the globe that are among the world's top innovators, market shapers, disruptors, including niche market leaders and regional champions."[40] Why, then, would the group position itself as a champion of Western values? What are these checks and balances they speak of? The prediction here seems to be that Western values will meet their logical limits, and what will remain will be some kind of "checks and balances." This talk of checks and balances has less to do with representing the interests of a constituency, and more to do with regulation. The WEF is manipulating the very definition of democracy to mean "regulation."

To be effective, such recommendations need to be implemented worldwide by every person on Earth. The WEF make it clear in their own reports: Agenda 21 proposes "an array of actions which are intended to be implemented by every person on Earth."[41] To succeed, this plan needs to be implemented not just at a national level, but at the local level. Rose Koire points this out in her book *Behind the Green Mask*, "Under the mask of green, our civil liberties are being restricted, constricted, and suffocated in every village and hamlet. The plan is imposed locally."[42] This effort to be implemented by every person is the reason the UN recommended every local government draft its own Agenda 21. This is the first chilling sign they meant this effort to be implemented in every corner of the world, and to elude any protections offered by elected officials or long-standing governments. Agenda 21 was designed to supersede sovereign borders. The framework of the UN's intentions is in the document itself. Chapter 7, paragraph 21 outlines how the UN will infiltrate local communities.

"Cities of all countries should reinforce cooperation among themselves and cities of the developed countries, under the aegis of non-governmental organizations active in this field, such as the International Union of Local Authorities (IULA), the International Council for Local Environmental Initiatives (ICLEI) and the World Federation of Twin Cities."[43]

So, what is the ICLEI? It purports to be concerned with smart growth and sustainable developments at the local level. The local level is the key. The ICLEI has been implemented in 2,500 cities, towns, and municipalities in 100 countries.[44] The council even has its own meeting every three years called the "World Congress of Local Governments for a Sustainable Future," and it includes over 200 governments from forty-three countries. This is troubling, as it is a means by which the UN can supersede elected officials at the national level, state, and local level. The UN can attempt to get around the laws that are meant to protect citizens and maintain sovereignty. The ICLEI reimagines where, how, and who gets to make certain decisions. By utilizing local officials like mayors, state senators, and aldermen, the UN can exert its influence without a national conversation, or reckoning of any kind, and it is all done in the name of sustainability.

A major tactic of this group is raising residential density—a goal that is returned to repeatedly in their literature. One example of a foundation aligned with this group is the Urban Land Institute,[45] whose study outlines recommendations for how to implement such a tactic.[46] While the scope of raising residential density is often presented ambiguously—with the implication that it could be as innocuous as adding an addition to a home, or a free-standing structure on a property—what the literature actually encourages, is the building of high-rise after high-rise in what was once a suburban neighborhood. A method in achieving this is to use what are sometimes called "impact fees" but are actually just taxes by another name. These impact fees may be used to coax people out of their own vehicles (especially when they are not Net-Zero-compliant, green-approved vehicles) and into public transport options and, in some cases, utilizing eminent domain to reappropriate private property for public use. These impact fees are one of the most insidious uses of climate change as justification for the state (or worse) to exert its power over individuals.

The ICLEI will use studies leveraging the excuse of sustainability to migrate citizens from rural, exurban, and suburban areas into densely populated city centers. According to the John Birch Society, this is all part of Agenda 2030's plan.

"Through high gas prices, implementation of the Paris Agreement, and manipulation of transportation patterns, the 2030 Agenda seeks to convince you, out of a desire to save money and avoid other inconveniences, that it would be expedient for you to move to more-developed and urban areas."[47]

Conclusion

Agenda 21 was drafted before most readers of this book were even born. The goals of it have been around for decades. These efforts to normalize austerity measures, to control the money supply, circumvent state sovereignty, and suppress individual freedoms are the fruits of the decades-long effort. Once the efforts of the ICLEI have crept into local elections, school board meetings, and home owners' associations, the global control of the UN and WEF will be complete. It is imperative that free-thinking individuals maintain awareness of these efforts to control everything from the money supply to the water supply. Once Davos-born economists can dictate the value of a worker's labor in places as far-flung as Buxton, North Carolina, East Sussex, England, and Okayama, Japan, and curtail their ability to buy a car or a home, the elites will have won.

The plan is to systematically control everything from food to money to energy, and finally, freedom. All must be slowly reduced to make people beg for the state's help. CBDC will be introduced via UBIs, and every single transaction and vaccine will be tracked via digital IDs and vaccine passports. These are the necessary evils to ensure the seventeen UN Sustainable Development Goals are delivered.

Chapter 9

Narrative Control

In the summer of 2020, the practice of knocking down statues became commonplace in the US. Initially, the practice was focused on monuments that lionized Confederate State heroes of the US Civil War, particularly monuments erected during the civil rights movements of the early 20th century.[1] Soon, however, the practice spread to include statues and monuments of America's founding fathers like Thomas Jefferson and George Washington, whose slaveholding practices had long been ignored in history books.[2] After a few months, however, even Abraham Lincoln, long held up as a symbol of the end to slavery in America because of the emancipation proclamation, became the focus of controversy, and his comments on race that did not match today's more enlightened sentiments, came to light.[3,4,5]

The practice spread from the US and became a global phenomenon.[6] The toppling and removing of statues, legally as well as extrajudicially, was so commonplace that when a statue of Frederick Douglass was toppled in Rochester, New York,[7] there was no consensus about why it was done or by whom. It could have been a response from the right to rankle left-wing agitators, or it could have been part of some effort to bring down cultural heroes and alliances and reframe the past through today's lens, all with the aim of ensuring adherence to the party/state.

Leaders in government and the mainstream media often excused or explained these attacks away, which has long been a tactic of dictators. The Cultural Revolution of Mao Zedong was centered on destroying what he considered the remnants of capitalism and traditionalism in China. The elites need to ensure their narratives are trusted with zero debate, so they dictate the story of how we came to this point, which is why they feel it necessary to erase parts of history. Once the story of history is properly sanitized and twisted to fit a modern narrative (usually the narrative that all of history has led to the current moment with the current leaders being the answer to some centuries-old equation), the present can be reframed. The current trends, as will be explored in this chapter, are to seed stories in the press, use fact-checkers and social media to dampen dissent, and hint at the future using predictive programming in the entertainment industry. Once the elites have power over the past, present, and future, there is nothing left to control.

The Hypocrisy of the Trusted News Initiative

Since the rise of the internet and the accompanying boom of independent media, legacy media outlets have been in a full-scale panic. Trust in mainstream news outlets has consistently plummeted over the past several decades. In an October 2021 GALLUP poll, twenty-nine percent of the US public registered "not very much" trust in the media.[8] This doubt may be due in part to everything from Nixon's Watergate scandal to the existence of weapons of mass destruction in Iraq. The mainstream news media worldwide has long done the bidding of governments and those in power. In 2019, a media conglomerate created the Trusted News Initiative (TNI).[9] This BBC-headed endeavor comprises major news organizations like Reuters and *The Washington Post*, along with social media companies such as Google, Meta, and Twitter. This bait and switch action creates a formal process for what was, prior to its inclusion, an unwritten rule. The TNI takes its marching orders from governments themselves, giving preferential treatment to information from the National Institute of Health, UN, FDA, CDC, and the WHO, when it is the true job of journalists to interrogate every press release, and question every premise and motive of these monolithic organizations.[10] Blind allegiance to government organizations is actually antithetical to the mission of the fourth estate. At one point, journalists saw themselves as a watchdog of government organizations and supranational groups like the UN. Now, the press releases from the TNI-linked organizations are supposedly trusted simply because of where they come from.

As if to hammer home how these endeavors become money-making efforts, Google created its own news initiative modeled on the TNI. Google is a publicly traded company whose goals are unabashedly to increase profits. They manage to check off various WEF-approved messaging elements by defining their goals as "strengthening quality journalism, supporting sustainable business models, and empowering newsrooms through technological innovation." By aiming to support sustainability, foster technological innovation, and ensure (vaguely defined) quality in journalism, they can justify all manner of profit-friendly decisions regarding what to highlight and what to de-emphasize. With a 300-million-dollar investment, Google must be hoping to achieve some kind of benefit for their shareholders.[11]

Who Checks the Fact-checkers?

One insidious tool of governments, mainstream media, and TNI proponents is what they call fact-checkers. Fact-checking has a complicated history, but what was once an attempt to make sense of a media landscape littered with lies and half-truths has become a new and wily way to advance propaganda agendas.

Snopes.com, for example, was created in the mid-1990s by a married couple who were interested in debunking urban legends and paranormal stories. As the site gained users, they expanded into the realms of geopolitics, history, law, and virology, to name a few. Upon the divorce of the couple two decades later, it was revealed that the fact-checkers hired people with no experience or credentials to be fact-checkers, and that they had no policy against bias. It resulted in *Forbes* calling the site a "black box that acts as the ultimate arbitrator of truth yet reveals little of its inner workings."[12] This was even before the plagiarism scandal.[13] It was too late, however. Facebook (now Meta) had acquired the flawed fact-check site to act as the referee of truth on their website(s).

Other fact-checking organizations have also come under fire for similar methodologically hollow practices of constructing "blacklisted" news si tes.[14] The Poynter Institute, a journalism school in Florida that has made itself a fact-checking juggernaut by running the International Fact-Checking Network and PolitiFact, gets its funding from some of the biggest media conglomerates and richest people on the planet, thus ensuring a conflict of interest.[15] With Bill Gates as a significant donor to the organization,[16] how can Poynter Institute possibly point out the questionable stories surrounding Gates' vaccination campaigns in India[17] and Africa,[18] or his continued misinformation regarding vaccination rates and herd immunity?

While Reuters, PolitiFact, Snopes, and other fact-checking agencies are quick to correct many of the negative stories about Bill Gates, Pfizer, Donald Trump, Joe Biden, Moderna, the CIA, the British Royal Family, Klaus Schwab, Henry Kissinger, and others in power, it is telling what they choose not to correct. Their other trick is in the framing; a common practice is to focus on only one element of a story and debunk the most outrageously false element of it—to paint the entire story as false when certain elements may be true. This is called the "poisoning the well" fallacy. One clear example of this is the "RFID microchip" story, which circulated throughout 2020. Some people in the west attributed their vaccine hesitancy to the possibility that vaccines contained microchips, and that Bill Gates wanted to track everyone by forcing them to take the vaccine.[19] The origin of this story is unclear, as is the number of people who believed it. Some more prominent fears that news outlets were less likely to fact-check were the perhaps well-founded fears that vaccine passports were being discussed as a way to track people in the future. People took notice when Yuval Noah Harari floated the idea to the *Financial Times* regarding everyone wearing wristbands in order to track sickness.[20] People certainly feared what might be in the vaccine and were hesitant because the vaccines had not been rigorously tested; Gates had created controversy with (aforementioned) vaccine efforts in the past, which had not gone well. It was much easier, however, for Reuters to isolate the most extreme views, destroy the most easily dismissible elements of said views and then, by suggestion and implication, dismiss the rest of the story. This is a very effective tactic for neutralizing a dissenting opinion. The FBI's surveillance and counter-espionage program COINTELPRO famously did this to Black civil rights leaders in the 50s and 60s with the edict "discredit, disrupt, destroy."[21]

Not only is Reuters using the playbook of spy agencies, but they also have a serious conflict of interest problem. James C. Smith, the chairman and former CEO of Reuters, is a major investor in Pfizer and is on the board of directors of both Pfizer and the WEF,[22] while he is also an executive at Reuters.[23] Not only is this conflict of interest not disclosed by Reuters, but even after this information came out, Poynter continued to endorse and recommend Reuters and their own fact-checking endeavors.[24]

Fact-checking itself is an endeavor that may be destined to fail, as humans are inherently biased. Throughout most political campaigns, people on every side of the debate will reframe information and data to suit their own perspectives. They will defend people who espouse their beliefs as being "taken out of context" when they say something untrue but will not give those from opposing perspectives the same latitude. In this way, fact-checking becomes biased and partisan theater, infinitely regressing arguments toward complete, fact-checked, partisan lies.[25]

As if all that was not bad enough, the British Army is getting in on the fact-checking game with the establishment of 77 Brigade in 2015, who aim to combat online disinformation with campaigns on Twitter, Facebook, etc.[26] According to their website, they use "nonlethal engagement and legitimate nonmilitary levers as a means to adapt behaviors of the opposing forces and adversaries." They seem to work very hard to avoid using the word propaganda here, but they might as well.

Not to be outdone, the US created its own state-sanctioned disinformation outlet: the Disinformation Governance Board (DGB) headed up by Nina Jankowicz, an unabashed musical theater fan who called herself "the Mary

Poppins of Disinformation."[27] This advisory board to the Department of Homeland Security (DHS) was met with immediate criticism.[28] The DGB was so controversial, they were forced to disband only weeks after being formed, but the damage had been done. Since the Twitter files have been released by Matt Taibbi, Elon Musk, et al., we have learned that the DGB was merely a formalization of the practices and the communication systems between state and private businesses that already existed. Indeed, the FBI, DHS, CIA, and powerful political operatives had been urging Twitter to silence dissenting voices for years.[29] This includes the silencing of people like the aforementioned Alex Berenson and the account of Zero Hedge who pushed the lab-leak theory, which is now a noncontroversial opinion.[30] Countless normal people, some with followings as small as a few dozen people, had their voices silenced because what they were saying was not in line with the accepted narrative. Far from being mere fact-checkers, these state organizations have enormous force, power, and resources behind them.

Unfortunately, once the DGB was dissolved, all the practices continued—just in secret—as Ken Klippenstein from *The Intercept* was able to uncover.[31] Key DHS documents revealed that even without the DGB, stories about Ukraine, racial justice, the US withdrawal from Afghanistan, and the true nature of the origins of COVID-19 were targeted. Klippenstein found that Facebook even created a special portal to make it easier for DHS to monitor these forms of speech.

Operation Mockingbird

Controlling the public through the media is nothing new. The CIA has been doing it for decades and they even have a name for it. It used to be called Operation Mockingbird, and like all CIA programs that were so effective, their work was discovered by curious, freedom-loving citizens. The CIA claimed Operation Mockingbird was a failure and had been discontinued, although it did continue in secret, just under a different name.

Legendary reporter Carl Bernstein (of Woodward and Bernstein fame) uncovered the secret. "The CIA admitted that at least 400 journalists and twenty-five large organizations around the world had secretly carried out assignments for the agency."[32] This operation was orchestrated so the CIA could dictate public opinion, but it did not stop with news journalists. Journalists were certainly useful when trying to mislead the public about some international, imperial endeavor, but there were other, more subtle manipulations happening as well. The CIA wanted to control the news cycle, but also the soft culture that was film, cinema, and even pop music. The CIA was not above putting lauded and award-winning writers like George Plimpton and Peter Mathieson on their payroll so they could monitor left-leaning individuals in the 1960s.[33] They also headed up an operation to distribute copies of the banned book *Doctor Zhivago*, a Nobel prize-winning Russian novel that celebrated the individual over the state, to Russians during the cold war. The success of the *Doctor Zhivago* operation may have led to the CIA sponsoring the creation of heavy metal band The Scorpions' monster hit "Winds of Change."[34] These are all examples of the CIA infiltrating entertainment in the US, abroad, and the media in order to shape public opinion. Operations such as these continue to this day, with the CIA still using many methods of control. They even have an office in Hollywood, which may have been used to insinuate themselves into hundreds of films. They have consulted on films as diverse as the factually inaccurate *Zero Dark Thirty*[35] to the seemingly benign comedy *Meet the Parents.*[36] Hollywood films are an imperative element of their agenda-setting, playing an important part in the maintenance of certain pieces of propaganda.

Why is this propaganda so important to the CIA? It goes back to another disavowed program—the program known as Project Monarch. What was the purpose of Project Monarch? It was a mass hypnosis campaign, which set out to control the minds of people and make them do what the state and the elites wanted them to do. What else could Hollywood be called but a mass hypnosis campaign?[37]

Who is the Victim?

It is hard to see the impact of these organizations and outlets when they are discussed in the abstract, but when dissenters are silenced and the lies of the establishment are foregrounded, there are real victims.

Michael Yeadon is a retired Pfizer executive who made claims about the risk Pfizer's vaccines could have on female fertility. While opponents claim his evidence is unfounded, the former Pfizer executive cites a German study that found lipid nanoparticles often found in vaccines can accumulate in the ovaries.[38] Although it is not disputed that lipid nanoparticles are used in COVID-19 shots, the critiques of Yeadon's assessment continued.[39] After leaked military data suggested an increase in miscarriages, Yeadon sought an apology from those who critiqued him. At the point of this book's publication, he has not yet received one.

Yeadon is not the only critic who had his name besmirched during the pandemic for trying to raise concerns about vaccines, but he was one of the most vocal. He was dubbed "the pandemic's wrongest man" by *The Atlantic* and was eventually permanently suspended from Twitter in 2021 for insisting things that were forbidden at the time.[40] Things such as the vaccines did not prevent transmission and were closer to therapeutic applications than vaccines. He did not even dispute the efficacy of the products. He merely had a semantic problem with calling them vaccines. He was proven to be right, of course, and he sued his way back onto the platform after it turned out that people like Joe Biden who claimed, "You're not going to get COVID if you have these vaccinations,"[41] were actually the ones spreading misinformation.

At this point, thousands of other people have been kicked off of Twitter for sharing COVID-19 misinformation.[42] That list does not, however, include people such as Joe Biden and the countless propagandists who repeated untrue information about the vaccine. Those labeled as "misinformants" are people who have had their careers derailed and their loyalties questioned. Some managed to navigate the tricky waters of deplatforming efforts, which were made by mega-powerful tech companies, who are actually in league with powerful governments and endlessly resourced pharmaceutical companies. There are other prominent figures who are not so lucky, and then there are the normal citizens of society at large, whose lives have been irreparably affected by the lies. Beyond the misinformed people who have taken vaccines that may harm them, or a voting public who might vote for what they might think is a righteous war but is actually a vicious land grab, there are those whose careers and lives are completely altered by these underhand tactics.

Threatening a dissident's career and their ability to speak freely seems to be only the beginning; the creeping increase of state control continues. In late 2022, PayPal, one of the largest online payment platforms in existence, updated its terms of service. Eagle-eyed consumers noticed something new in the terms: a $2,500 fine for users who share messages that are "fraudulent, promote misinformation, or are unlawful."[43] This vague language and hefty fine caught the attention of many and resulted in a mass exodus of people, worried they could receive a bill in the mail for repeating President Joe Biden's claim that the vaccine protected against transmission... or for stating the opposite. With no explanation from PayPal over who would make the determination if a statement was fraudulent, illegal, or promoted misinformation, users were unsurprisingly worried. PayPal was quick to amend this, calling it a mistake, but that opens up a new question. Is making a mistake acceptable to users of PayPal? If they were to make a mistake like Joe Biden did when he said the vaccine would protect from infection, would they still be subject to the fine? These questions remained unanswered, and the policy was quietly reinstituted after being rescinded.[44] This opens up a scary new avenue for compliance. If PayPal can begin fining its users for "misinformation," can banks? Can Twitter? How about a Chinese company like TikTok? Might they be able to bill an entire nation of teenagers and financially hobble a generation? It sounds absurd, but so does a $2,500 fine from a banking app for sharing an article written by the New York Times.

Conclusion

Where does this leave us? Silenced? Perhaps not. What is happening is all happening out in the open. Being informed is one of the best salves against the encroaching totalitarianism of these efforts. Seeing things like the DGB and the TNI for what they really are is important, but often by the time you see what is happening, it is already done. There may be another method for protecting yourself from the state. There is an idea that while the elites control the narrative on a global level, there is a way to predict what might come to pass.

First, thinkers like George Orwell back in the 1940s laid out the blueprint for the kind of state control we see. He knew surveillance was inevitable, and the easier it was to surveil the citizens, the more likely the state would be to do it. Everything from the language in the news media to the way self-censorship heads dissent before it happens was warned about in Orwell's prescient novel.[45] Other works of fiction provide warnings for where society may be going or may already be. This includes the work of P.K. Dick, particularly with the concept of "thought crimes" in his story "Minority Report,"[46] and Neal Stephenson, who coined the term "Metaverse" in his 1992 novel *Snow Crash*.[47]

But these guesses, however ornate and attention-grabbing, may not be the only way to suss out warnings.[48] Scholars from Ohio State,[49] along with academics publishing in the International Journal of Semiotic Law,[50] have studied this phenomenon and come to some arresting conclusions. These studies suggest that by priming the public's imagination, it prepares us for coming changes. We need to seed ideas about wars or plagues or famines and get the public to reckon with these realities first, so their opinions and actions already have momentum, ultimately making them easier to control. There is another possibility for why the elites may use predictive programming, and it is far stranger than anything studied by the Ohio State University. It has to do with mass rituals and ancient order, and it all sounds pretty hard to believe until you trace things from the "beginning" to the present day. The next chapter explores the link from Ancient Rome all the way to the WEF today.

Chapter 10

The Global Control Matrix

How did it come to this? How could a few individuals at the top suddenly seize control in the middle of the 20th century, and then reshape the past and the present to control the future? The answer is they did not. None of this is new. This chapter will explore some of the oldest controlling groups in the world. It will look at how they gained power, and how they still wield it today. As the history of these groups is explained, their links to current power structures will become apparent.

In this chapter, we briefly highlight the ancient societies and orders that are rumored to still control the world today. When you look at the connections to lower-tier organizations, key people, and other supranational organizations, their influence is hard to deny. From The Crown (Temple) to the Council on Foreign Relations, from the Freemasons to the CIA, from Kissinger to Schwab, the ancient and ever-expanding reach of the global order will be explored.

Mystery Religions

Mystery religions, followed by the most powerful people in a society, may have their roots in Atlantean times, but more certainly with hunter-gatherers who relied on the sun for life. This system of thought adhered to a secret set of beliefs and philosophies, particularly associated with evolution, the sun, and the night. This is why the Illuminati worshipped the light. Christianity is perceived by the worshipers of this mystery religion as a perversion of their belief system. The Egyptian version of this worships the figure Horus, who is seen as the savior of mankind and whose name remains today in the word "hours" and the word "horizon." Indeed, the power of this mystery religion is so great that we still feel its impact today, even if we do not know it.

Over the centuries, mystery religions spread out to every corner of the world and influenced religion in far-flung places such as Mexico, Ireland, and the US. The symbols of these religions show up in statues, currency, churches, advertising, and governmental buildings all over the world, and secret societies like the Order of the Quest, Freemasonry, the Ancient Order of the Rose and Cross, The Knights Templar, the Sovereign and Military Order of the Knights of Malta, the Order of Saint John of Jerusalem, the Skull and Bones, and the Illuminati. They all have their roots in this ancient belief system.

Mystery Babylon

Thanks to the work of Ralph Woodrow's *Babylon Mystery Religion*[1] and Alexander Hislop's *The Two Babylons*,[2] the connections between these ancient philosophies and Christianity are now known. The rituals of these ancient pagan religions, specifically Babylonian religions, are carried on throughout Christian faiths, specifically in Catholicism. The work of these scholars has revealed that everything from the construction of temples to the worship of mother and child to the emblem of the cross was adopted from earlier pagan religions. This is the way these symbols and rituals persist. They are smuggled into other belief systems and presented as something they are not, thus indoctrinating and controlling millions of people over centuries.

Rome turns out to be a central figure in this story, with many seeing Catholicism as the "whore of Babylon" mentioned in the Book of Revelations.[3] But Rome is just the modern representation of a mystery school that most likely arrived with them from the Greeks, the Ancient Egyptians, and before them, the "lost civilization" of the Atlanteans with their purported "god-like" knowledge and seemingly impossible powers.[4]

This potential subversion emerges in religious orders and organizations throughout history, and, as we mentioned in the introduction, the greatest empire of the past, The Romans were allowed to present their version of history as fact. Is it possible that the crusades, conquistadors, and English witch trials, etc., were merely purges of ancient, maybe forbidden knowledge, to ensure the doctrine of Christianity was enforced globally on behalf of the ruling dynasty?

Jesuits

One religious order whose origins are questionable is the Jesuits, which is seen as the military arm of the Vatican. St. Ignatius Loyola founded the Jesuit order in 1534 in Spain. Loyola was a soldier wounded in a battle against the French. While healing, he founded The Society of Jesus, later known as The Jesuit Order or simply as The Jesuits.[5] It was Loyola's military background that formed the somewhat imperial nature of his order, and the group made its way into various places and career paths, as opposed to simply operating out of the church.

Loyola's military background is also what led to him creating the position of the "Superior General of the Society of Jesus." This position is sometimes referred to as the "Black Pope." The incumbent is responsible for the exclusively male religious order, thus donning the black clothing commonly associated with a priest. According to catholic.com, he is called the Black Pope "because he wore the Jesuits' black clerical garb, in contrast to the real pope, who wore white and became known as 'the White Pope.'"[6]

Throughout the 16th and 17th centuries, the Jesuits continued to expand their order. They came to the shores of England where they continued their mission of spreading Catholicism to England, Scotland, and Wales, where it was illegal.[7] They entered China through Portuguese settlements to engage in missionary work, and they spread to Canada and the US.[8]

One Roman dynastic family reputedly rules them all: The Orsini Family. This family's roots can be traced back as far as Rome in 998 and possibly even as far back as Nimrod, a biblical figure mentioned in the Book of Genesis. Since the election of Giacinto Orsini as Pope in 1191, they have been intrinsically linked to the papacy. The Orsini clan has enriched itself over the centuries by operating in proximity to the powerful Catholic church, with many descendants of the clan earning high positions in the papacy. The pro-papal household found themselves in a centuries-long feud with the pro-imperial Colonna family, and this feud would shape the families, laws of Rome, and the papacy for years to come. The Orsini family found themselves aligned with the Guelph faction of the Italian political system, who opposed the German-based, Holy Roman Empire-aligned Ghibelline family. The Guelph dynasty can be traced back to the German dukes of Bavaria.[9]

The most powerful person in the world may not be whom most people think. If the theory of the Black Pope is correct, it means The Superior General of the Jesuits controls "the White Pope," most supernational organizations like the CFR, the Bilderberg Group, and the Council of Trent as well as secret societies like the Freemasons, various intelligence agencies like the CIA (also known as Catholics in Action), Mossad, and MI5, and the highest branches of government. Today's incumbent is Father Arturo Sosa Abascal, and the lineage goes back to the 16th century in Spain when the Black Pope was established. These systems of control go back that far and their reach spreads that wide.[10] Given the fact both the White and Black Popes are deemed "commoners" and not of dynastic decent, it is rumored (although difficult to prove) that a "Grey Pope" exists, who is the ultimate ruling "king" of the world. Could it be an Orsini?

The Sovereign Order of Malta

The Sovereign Order of Malta has its roots in 1048, when merchants from the maritime republic of Amalfi gained permission to build a church, convent, and hospital in Jerusalem, with the stated purpose of caring for and protecting pilgrims on their way to what they considered the holy land. In 1113, the Pope officially recognized them as a lay-religious order of the Catholic Church. During the crusades, the Sovereign Order of Malta evolved from a hospital to a military organization. Following the defeat and ousting of crusaders in Jerusalem, the Order relocated to Cyprus, and the Catholic Church officially recognized it as a sovereign authority.

This sovereignty makes the Order an interesting and unique group on the international stage, and they are often considered a country with no territory, though they have dabbled with empire-building. At one time, the Order controlled several Caribbean islands. Their current headquarters are in Rome and their buildings are treated similarly to a foreign embassy. The Sovereign Order of Malta has its own currency, passports, stamps, and license plates. Over 100 nations recognize the Order as a sovereign entity and, importantly, they are recognized by the UN as having permanent observer status, not unlike the Vatican.[11] Many founders of the CIA were Knights of Malta, including William Donovan, "the father of the CIA,"[12] along with the "father of the FBI," Charles Joseph Bonaparte.[13]

As mentioned before, it is believed the Grey Pope controls the Sovereign Order of Malta, and his power exceeds that of both the White and the Black Pope, who are both considered "commoners." The King of Spain is reputedly the Roman Monarch of the World and the Sovereign Order of Malta Military Navigator, possibly making him the second most powerful man in the world.[14]

The Order of the Garter

This group was formed by King Edward III to reflect the chivalry of the knights of King Arthur. The group is supposed to honor people who distinguish themselves with their public service.[15] What is notable about the Order of the Garter is the mythology that surrounds it. It is an organization that has its roots in the story of Richard III, who protected the order of a young lady after she dropped her garter by attaching the garment to his own leg and stating that "soon everyone would be proud to wear garters."[16] This story behind the formation of the group has been much mocked and maligned in popular media, dating at least as far back as the 19th century, which frustrated the British Monarchy in the "failure of the Order's official historians to control its mythical associations with women and sex."[17] The apocryphal incident covers for the fact that it may go back to an ancient Babylonian ritual of emasculating a king by forcing him to wear garments meant for a woman. In 2022, Tony Blair was appointed as a Knight Companion to the Order of the Garter despite petitions to the UK Government to stop it, given his questionable Iraq War justifications and leadership. Was this his reward?

The Crown (Temple)

Not unlike the Sovereign Order of Malta, the Crown (Temple) also has its roots in the crusade. It, too, was a small military organization fighting against those they perceived as infidels. They protected Christian pilgrims and made their headquarters the location of King Solomon's temple. In the early 12th century, the group acquired territory throughout the holy land and Europe. Also, like the Sovereign Order of Malta, it was important to be recognized by the Vatican. Having been thusly deputized, the Crown (Temple) set about making themselves the defenders of Christian artifacts, almost akin to some kind of archeological acquisition agents.

This organization spread and created an entire bureaucracy and infra-structure, which included the Mason brothers. The Masons were laymen brought in to carry out tasks the Crown needed completing. At first, it was simply masonry, but it soon expanded to include other jobs. This subset of the group is what many believe to be the origin of the Fraternal Order of Freemasons.

One of the key contributions of the Templars was the creation of a banking system, which allowed money to be more easily stored, cataloged, and transported in and out of the holy land. Since silver and gold were cumbersome and heavy, the Templars created encrypted password systems and notes of credit that could be redeemed and exchanged at various locations. The fees charged for this service created enormous wealth for the group.[18]

Soon, the Knights of the Order of the Templar created alliances that increased their power and wealth, rather than a supposed mission statement. Inevitably, this led to confessions of worship of an idol referred to as Baphomet, yet more evidence of a secret society whose rituals could be traced back to Babylonian paganism and the Mystery Schools. Crown (Temple) is reputed to still control the finances of the ruling dynasty, and remains within the City of London Corporation. "The Monarch aristocrats of England have not been ruling sovereigns since the reign of King John, circa 1215. All royal sovereignty of the old British Crown since that time has passed to the Crown Temple in Chancery."[19]

The Order of Rose Croix

The Order of the Rose Croix, also known as the Kabbalistic Order of the Rose Cross, has its roots all the way back in the 1500s, with the symbol of a rose and a cross supposedly coming from the family crest of Martin Luther. Since then, the order acquired various influence including that of the Kabbalah and a practice called Rosicrucianism as well as the enlightenment philosophies of 18th century France, which was when many of the traditions of the Order were formalized.

The Order of Rose Croix is a select group inside the group we now know today as Freemasons. Members of Freemasonry are expected to complete certain rites to gain privilege and prestige within the group. The 18th degree is only conferred upon candidates who are "princes" of the organization. It is a high honor and those with the distinction find themselves in an elite club. The degrees of the Order hint at the ancient nature of the group; a member progresses through the degrees of conferment, symbolically experiencing the Order as it was during the Old Testament through to the New Testament and on to the New Covenant.[20] The candidates of this group perform various ceremonies and complete various rites. It places members in a very enviable position within the organization and hints at how important they can be both inside it and out. To get a sense of how much power someone in this group can wield, one need only look at the members of this fraternity. They include Theodore Roosevelt, Benjamin Franklin, Henry Ford, and Colin Powell.[21]

The Fabians, Rhodes Scholars, and the Milner Round Table

Elites created the Fabian Socialist Society in the wake of the monopolistic British East India company, which was dismantled by regulation in 1873. The British shareholders of this company, which traded tea and silk along with opium and slaves, had become extremely wealthy. They later formed The Fabian Socialistic Society to conduct spiritual research and reconstruct society in accordance with the highest moral possibilities. The Fabians worked with thinkers, journalists, and artists to push socialist propaganda and urge English citizens to become socialists. One member, Sidney Webb, founded the London School of Economics (handily located opposite the Temple Bar area of London) with the help of some usual suspects of the 19th and 20th century elitism: namely the Rockefeller Foundation, the Carnegie United Kingdom Trust, and the Morgan family.

Webb became a leader in the Labor party, thus the seeds of control from the British East India Company to the halls of parliament were traced.

Beyond economists and politicians, Fabians used prominent playwrights and novelists, such as George Bernard Shaw and H. G. Wells, to present their agenda to the public. One such tome was Wells' *Modern Utopia* (1905),[22] which, not unlike the tenets of the WEF, was sponsored by a wealthy industrialist, Graham Wallas, and has its origin in a conference in the Swiss Alps. This effort funded by ancient money was designed to control the minds and opinions of the citizenry. Wells was friends with Edward Bernays, grandson of Sigmund Freud, and the man who literally wrote the book on propaganda. Bernays is famous for advocating for the manipulation of the public, as is evidenced in this now-infamous quote.

"As civilization becomes more complex, and as the need for invisible government has been increasingly demonstrated, the technical means have been invented and developed by which public opinion may be regimen ted."[23]

Eventually, the Fabian society expanded to include other prominent members of society such as Bertrand Russell, a philosopher enamored with the idea of socialism, John Dewey, who is responsible for the establishment of the progressive education system, Upton Sinclair, and many other notable names.

Cecil Rhodes was a financier of South African diamond mines and as he came to the end of his life, he established a scholarship in his will that would establish "... a secret society with but one object—the furtherance of the British Empire and the bringing of the whole uncivilized world under British rule, for the recovery of the United States, (and) for... making the Anglo-Saxon race but one Empire."[24] It is unclear if the founder of the Rhodes Scholarship, Cecil Rhodes, was a member of the Fabian society, but Oxford University was, and Rhodes established his scholarship through Oxford University. The Fabian Society took control of the Rhodes Scholarship and began using it to indoctrinate a generation of thinkers, politicians, and influencers.[25] This is the same tactic that has been outlined elsewhere in the book regarding Harvard's International Seminar and WEF's Young Global Leaders program. This tactic has long been a cornerstone for swaying public debate and squashing dissent among those outside the ruling class.

The Rhodes Scholarship also led to the Milner Group. Alfred Milner actually decided how the scholarship would be administered and is, in many ways, its architect, despite it being named after Rhodes. The inner circle of the Milner Group became known as Milner's Kindergarten. Some members of this group include Dean Rusk, a member of the Council on Foreign Relations and Secretary of State in the US from 1961 to 1969, General Wesley Clark Commander of the NATO forces in Europe from 1997 to 2000, and former president of the US, Bill Clinton. Milner is responsible for *The Round Table*, a publication offering foreign policy viewpoints favorable to British expansion and internationalism.

As is so often the case with many of these groups, they overlapped with other organizations, rebranded many times, and some powerful members within these groups formed their own groups. For example, they often referred to the Milner Group as the Round Table Group. Both the Royal Institute of International Affairs (also known as Chatham House) and the CFR have similar strong links with the Round Table Group. The CFR was a group established in New York and was considered a "sister organization" to the Milner Group.[26]

Through it all, Rome has been the keeper of this ancient religion and this ancient set of rules. During history, Rome has demanded tribute from all over the globe, including from England and Ireland.[27] Meanwhile, Freemasonry has spread throughout the American colonies and people like George Washington, Benjamin Franklin, Alexander Hamilton, and John Hancock were spreading the iconography and philosophy of the mystery religion in the founding of Washington, D.C.[28] Many buildings in D.C. emulate famous buildings in Rome, such as the Eccles Building of the Federal Reserve, the White House, and the Lincoln Memorial. Is Washington D.C. the new Babylon?

Conclusion

There is some speculation that the ultimate control exists with a ruling dynasty—royalty in the shadows derived from an ancient group of thirteen families with deep ties to ancient Rome, and possibly even further back to the times of Ancient Greece. Considering Rome was the first true Empire, it's not impossible to imagine that the mystery religions spread throughout Rome and beyond, and ancient cultural and family loyalties still wield the ultimate power today. We can postulate this from those who command the top tier control mechanisms such as the Sovereign Order of Malta, the Order of the Croix, the Order of the Garter, the Jesuits, and the Fabian Society.

When the tendency toward public-private partnership is examined, the tactics and influence of these ancient orders can be traced.[29] This broad and ancient endeavor is about power, and it always has been. The seat of control has evolved from churches, monasteries, and oracles to nongovernmental agencies, global corporations, and philanthropic foundations.

Chapter 11

Bias Check - What if "They" are Right?

This book has asserted many claims. It is important that any exceptional claim has exceptional evidence. Individuals should explore extraordinary claims they encounter and consider them against other points of view. It is the duty of the individual to do this to avoid being either tricked into belief systems that contradict their values, or convinced of something that turns out to be untrue.

This chapter explores some of the bigger claims made in this book and considers dissenting opinions. What good is any idea if it does not hold up to scrutiny? Could it be that some ideas explored by the mainstream media are actually warranted? Is there evidence-based research out there regarding COVID-19, the vaccines, or climate change? This chapter aims to find out.

The UN is a Toothless Organization with No Real Power in the World

While it may be tempting to cast the UN as a nefarious organization bent on world domination, particularly when they collaborate with groups like the WEF, the reality is much more nuanced. The UN can claim some measurable successes over the past few decades. This facility for international discussion has accomplished various large projects for the betterment of the world. This includes facing major global issues like the spread of HIV/AIDS and polio, reducing child mortality and reducing hunger. These are objectives that have measurable results. Since 2001, there has been a fifty-two percent reduction in HIV infections in children and a one-third reduction in adult populations. Polio has been all but eradicated on a global level. Child mortality has been almost cut in half, and the International Fund for Agricultural Development (IFAD) has reduced hunger significantly.[1]

Defenders of the UN present the organizations as merely a platform for powerful actors on the world stage to come together and address problems that would otherwise not be addressed. In this way, it is a net positive for the global population.

While some detractors may concede the UN has benefited some people, other critics of the UN's efforts find the results to be underwhelming. While child mortality, polio, AIDS deaths and hunger have been reduced, these critics see this as resulting from other efforts, as the UN's primary goal is often to maintain peace in a world beset by war. As a peacekeeping organization, it is hard to laud the UN as a success story. The UN has almost systematically failed to prevent wars like the Vietnam War, the conflict in Yemen, the Syrian Civil War, and many others.[2] This speaks to the UN's lack of power and its lack of effectiveness.

While this may be a critique of the UN, it is a pretty strong indicator they may not actually be able to maneuver the world into the shape they want it to be. If they cannot adhere to their own very basic mission statement as a peacekeeping operation, then how could they possibly exert their power over the rest of the world?

While this is a compelling argument, it also includes the seeds of its refutation. The effectiveness of the UN's inoculation campaigns is a large part of how they exert their control. Their very successes as a distributor of HIV and polio medicine are only possible because of its relationship with drug manufacturers, and its ability to manipulate the world food supply speaks to the way it uses its partnerships in every corner of the world. They can use these successes as bargaining chips to indorse policies they want enacted. Their supposed inability to stop wars is, again, proof of their influence. They do not stop the wars because they do not want to stop the wars. It is as simple as that. The people who pull the strings and fund the organization are often in a position to benefit when wars continue to rage. The UN has shown that it can throw its influence around when they want to, but it will not do so if its interference would fail to benefit certain benefactors.

Davos is Nothing but a Pageant

The critics of the WEF make similar claims about the efficacy of the WEF as they do about the UN. The WEF is a spectacle where the wealthiest want to be invited to the exclusive club. While it may be a very fertile networking opportunity for certain world business leaders, it is not some agenda-setting forum, but rather an end-of-year party.

One man often mentioned in the same breath as the other wealthy participants of Davos is Elon Musk. Musk compared the meeting to 4Chan, the online message board full of posturing, positioning, and toxicity. He famously turned down an invitation to Davos and explained that it was not because the group "engaged in diabolical scheming," but because the event sounded boring.[3]

Musk is far from the only one calling out Davos, with CNN[4] and CNBC[5] also joining in on calling Davos and the WEF irrelevant and mostly bad at predicting the future. CNN points out the fact that while Trump attended in the past, Joe Biden skipped the 2023 meeting, along with China's Xi Jinping and other world leaders who previously participated.

It is possible the WEF is a relic of the neoliberal effort towards globalization. With supply chain issues forcing manufacturers and businesses to think locally rather than globally, and the "Golden Arches Theory" (where two countries each with a McDonald's would have no reason to go to war with one another) being proven incorrect, we may see the first indications of neoliberalism's failure on the global stage. If this is true, however, how much more dangerous would that make the WEF? A trapped animal is the most dangerous type of animal. What kind of damage could the WEF cause if its power wanes?

The Great Reset is a Talking Point for Neoliberalism and Not a Vast Conspiracy

Speaking of neoliberalism as a philosophy, the WEF comes across as yet another laboratory for neoliberal ideology to thrive. Certainly, having Harvard, the CIA, and Henry Kissinger as sponsors of the organization, speaks to a neoliberal bent toward their philosophies. Neoliberalism is, of course, the twentieth-century-born philosophy centered on global free market trade. It has been instituted by many powerful world leaders, including Margaret Thatcher and Ronald Reagan. The idea relies heavily upon the work of economists Friedrich von Hayek and Milton Friedman, who believed in laissez-faire approaches to regulation.[6]

The WEF fits the criteria of neoliberalism well. They make no secret about their belief in the market. They claim it is a great equalizer and can lift people out of poverty, though that claim has been challenged as a disingenuous justification for accumulating wealth and power.

Interestingly, the WEF has tried to separate themselves from such a label, with the WEF going so far as to call for the "end of neoliberalism."[7] This approach has often been derided by critics of the WEF, who point out that the WEF's "entire business model has always rested on providing megacorporations with a PR shield to pretend that they aim to do better."[8] This critique calls out the WEF as neoliberalism by another name and longs for democratic nations to work in opposition to groups like the WEF.

Regardless of semantics, critics of the WEF's overreach are seeing the same thing as most people who are concerned with the Great Reset. Just as neoliberalism has little to do with liberalism, Klaus Schwab's efforts to distance his organization from the term do not prove that his aims are any different from dogged proponents of the ideology like Tony Blair and Bill Clinton. What these people are seeking is an attempt to gain power and to use that power in new and frightening ways.

The Pandemic was a Triumph of Government Mobilization and Scientific Problem-solving

The response to the COVID-19 pandemic was beset by problems and mistakes. Almost no one will argue in good faith that every decision made was correct. The mistakes have been well-chronicled: information was not properly disseminated, some reactions were overzealous, and some assumptions about the vaccine were wrong. Overall, it was a triumph of international cooperation, scientific know-how, and mobilization.

The vaccine was created, manufactured, and distributed for use in under a year. Mitigation efforts were quickly enacted, including the use of masks, testing, and instituting new health standards and social norms. Relief aid was distributed, and while they instituted quarantines and lockdowns, the efforts to reinstitute travel, get children back to school, and put people back to work were just as impressive as the lockdown efforts. Not only that, but better preparedness efforts and supply chain measures were instituted.

People learned from the crisis and rose to the challenge. The instinct to criticize and belittle certain efforts that were failures undermines the success of the endeavor in its entirety. But these points just underscore the vast power of the elites and pharmaceutical juggernauts who spearheaded the response. It is specifically the ability to mobilize to respond to such a situation that reveals the vast reach of those in power.

Climate Change

Climate change is one of the most severe and bitter debates had in today's already polarized world. For every pro, there is a con. For every argument, there is a rebuttal.

While scientists still debate nuances and particulars, they all seem to agree on recent warming trends. Certainly, there are cycles of heating and cooling over the history of the Earth which undermines recent increases, but the rate at which the planet has heated over the past century is unprecedented. It is not untrue that certain businesses and industries rely on climate change narratives, and that governments can misuse the narrative to force compliance, but all this does not mean climate change is not manmade.[9]

They can argue these claims back and forth, but what both sides of the argument miss is where the opposing groups overlap. Climate change activists are deeply suspicious of fossil fuel manufacturers. There is a resounding call among climate change activists to push back against the power of the fossil fuel industry. These calls are surprisingly similar to those who are suspicious of the WEF's locus of control.

So often, climate change discussion is hijacked by PR firms and the hypocritical elites, who are fine telling peasants to start a compost heap while they travel around the world on their private jets. Climate change activists and skeptics have more in common than they think, and if they were to stop arguing with one another and resist the powerful interests of fossil fuel companies, they might each get what they are looking for.

Do Bugs Cure Cancer?

While eating insects may seem disgusting to anyone who has not grown up with the practice, eating bugs as an extra source of protein may become common practice in the western, developed world when traditional sources of protein like chicken and beef become more and more expensive to produce.[10] Opponents of this practice cite health risks of eating bugs, like chitin's potential for triggering allergic responses, as well as a potentially cancer-causing agent, but there may be health benefits as well. Some initial studies have found that chitin may be a potential treatment for cancer.[11] Studies of this sort are in the very early stages, so it is unclear at this point which direction it will go. The important thing to follow with this issue is to make sure the food supply is robust enough to support the populace. How governments, individuals, and companies go about this remains to be seen.

CBDC as a Safeguard Against Crypto Scams

Since the rise of cryptocurrency markets, users have been targets of scams. Cryptocurrency scams abound with investors being warned of fake wallets, pyramid scams, Ponzi schemes, pump & dumps, and fraudulent Initial Coin Offerings.[12] Sam Bankman-Fried made international headlines for the way his web of corporations defrauded customers,[13] but he is only one of many potential crypto-fraudsters who have profited from the pain of others. It almost seems like the wild west of digital currencies could use a sheriff to regulate massively powerful players who would exploit its users in ways hitherto unimagined. This is one of the most compelling arguments for CBDC. While the dollar currently has the reputation as one of the world's most stable forms of currency, those who want to institute CBDC see increased potential for those currencies as well, in that digital programming affords the central banks far reaching controls on how and when digital currencies are used compared to cash. Whilst many alternative coin holders argue the strengths of decentralization for digital currencies, detractors contend that the very centralization and built-in controls of CBDC prevent the criminality and tax evasion associated with cash.

UBI is the Opposite of Austerity

While UBI is critiqued by some as the ultimate in socialism, some argue that UBI could actually free many people from the poverty caused by austerity measures.[14] While governments would retain control in the levels of UBI paid, the scheme has the potential to be a powerful and direct tool for reducing and possibly eliminating poverty. Instilling the fear of poverty into citizens, is one of the key manipulation tactics of government. Taking away one's job and reducing access to wealth have traditionally been ways for the powerful to control the weak. By providing citizens a regular income, government effectively nullify one of their own key control mechanisms. For example, the efficacy of mask wearing and vaccine mandates were regularly debated throughout the COVID-19 pandemic. Such mandates would have been much harder to impose on the workforce if the backstop of a regular income from the government negated their need for mask compliance at work.

One of the key elements of controlling inflation is what central banks call the "Non-Accelerating Inflation Rate of Unemployment" or NAIRU. In a monetarist-based economy such as the US and UK today, the NAIRU needs to run between five and six percent for inflation to be kept at the central bank target rate of two percent. In effect, this means that economies *need* five to six percent of the population unemployed to keep inflation in check. This is a product of wage demands feeding through into higher inflation. UBI levels the playing field and proponents of MMT argue that the natural rate of interest rates would then be zero percent.

Ancient Orders

There is something tautological about listing ancient orders as proof of their prominence. There have always been ancient orders. Elites always scramble for power. Rituals are always used to commemorate and celebrate power and prestige. That the sun or triangles emerge in many religions and secret societies just speaks to the enduring power of these symbols, not to the secret political power of the ancient orders.

Most religions emerge from a need for order and explanations in an irrational world. Myths emerge among cultures and those myths are ritualized, passed down, and utilized throughout generations. Often religions exist to explain death, to give life meaning, and to codify a system of morality that is acceptable to a group. Religious scholars have identified some common aspects of major religions including the belief in a supreme being, reverence for set sacred writings and ideas, as well as the importance of a type of pilgrimage to a holy land or to spread the faith in the religion.[15]

Religious iconography also often has to do with the sky and the sun, as most religions predate many modern conveniences. The sun and the weather had more to do with the lives of ancient farmers since they could not rely on international shipping and refrigeration to keep them alive during a drought. They worshipped the sun and prayed for rain because these two factors played a much larger role in their lives than they do in a modern person's life.

These commonalities are not evidence of a grand conspiracy linking the religions to one another. The common aspects of these religions actually prove the opposite. It is an example of various groups organizing themselves in similar ways despite the lack of contact rather than because of it.

These commonalities do not disprove the existence of powerful people using the church as a cover for their misdeeds, but it does make one element of the accusation shakier. To prove that Babylonian rituals were co-opted by Catholic leadership to continue an ancient and mysterious religion, one would need more proof than merely the similarity between rituals. Whilst it is curious how many world leaders are a part of secret societies, it does not prove their intentions. It is certainly notable, however.

The Age of Information

While it is true that world leaders are forever trying to suppress information that is inconvenient to their grand plans and power grabs, there is an argument to be made that they are failing to do so in any meaningful way. While the mainstream media continues to collapse[16] and independent news outlets grow in power and influence, the public has more access to information than ever before.

Even as the government tries to scrub the internet of its most damning information, or to pump out so much misinformation that the truth is obscured, it cannot be denied that we live in an age of unprecedented access to information. Much of what we now know about the lies of the media, the profit motives of the pharmaceutical companies, or the ways world leaders are compromised, were completely hidden in generations past. They are now immediately available to anyone who wants to know the truth.

Conclusion

Just as the claims made by prominent people in the media and the government should be scrutinized, so should the claims in this book. If any of the claims made in this book seem unfathomable or false, it is easier than ever to locate the truth. All one needs to do is learn to be savvy enough to separate the truth from the lies. If you are capable of that, the lies of the media cannot lead you astray. You are invited to investigate any and all of the extraordinary claims in this book. The only way to get to the truth is if everyone makes this a habit. To dismiss a claim out of hand as false is a logical fallacy that no critical thinker should engage in. You will not find your way to the truth by utilizing ad hominem attacks, straw man arguments, equivocation, or appeal to authority. Too often these tactics are used to lead people astray and readers should be wary of such practices.

Chapter 12

The Great Resistance

This book has argued for several chilling and pessimistic claims. It has sewn distrust for the highest levels of government and industry. It has made accusations against some very powerful people, and it has shown itself to be incredibly cynical when it comes to international organizations, the government, academia, the media, and the healthcare industry. However, this book is not meant to be entirely hopeless. Quite the opposite. This book is meant to inform and act as a societal call to action. It is meant to enlighten, and it is meant to shine a light on potential dangers so they can be avoided.

What follows will differ from the rest of the book. While it will not be a step-by-step guide for how to emerge from the morass, it will shine a light on what can be done to extricate oneself from the clutches of the powerful. The systems of control are sometimes so ingrained that it is easy to miss them. The elites have pulled the strings for so long, we tend to take some of their programming for granted. While participation in government is often pointed to as a way to make a change, there is a way to do it that is effective and a way to do it that is ineffective. While we all know that indoctrination is bad, how can education be weaponized against this reality? Certainly, the pharmaceutical industry is not to be trusted, but where can one turn when we are sick? These issues are difficult to address, but an attempt will be made in this chapter to do so. As any life coach will ask you when approaching a problem, "what are you trying to achieve by taking this course of action?" This book has presented many of the problems, but what about presenting some possible solutions? How can wider society take action and force the elites to change course? We outline a few suggestions in the following, but the list is by no means exhaustive.

Less Government

If the supernational organizations like the UN and WEF want to control the populations at the local governmental level through the ICLEI, then the first and most obvious battleground for the future of the soul of humanity is at the local governmental level. Citizens have little hope of engaging with strategic thinkers and billionaires, but they do have a voice at the local, municipal level working from the bottom up. If every town and city started action plans against bogus climate change narratives, like fifteen-minute zone implementations, then the base of the power pyramid could be undermined leading to corrupted power structures being toppled.

There are various plans in place to counter the top-down governmental style of most western style governments and to empower people at the lower level to decentralize the structure of governance. One nation that has a very strong effort to localize governments is the UK, where the fight for autonomy has been raging for generations. The former British Empire has lessened its control abroad, but its more local incursions (Ireland, Scotland, and Wales) have long had an acrimonious relationship with the British crown. Recently, efforts to further wrest control from centralized

English power have emerged.[1] These efforts focus on moving away from technocracy and toward democracy—empowering local governments to enact the type of change that is good for the people in the area, not just good for the elites.

Efforts to localize government are not limited to the UK, as politically aware people have been mobilizing in significantly higher numbers since the beginning of the 21st century. Indeed, participating in strengthening local representation is a good way to take back some of the power national and supranational organizations exert over individuals. Local governments make decisions about school budgets, police budgets, and local health efforts. Local government is where high ideals meet the implementation, which is why the UN is so interested in efforts to spread the reach and control of the ICLEI. One sure-fire way to oppose the spread of this effort is to "be there and be informed" when they show up, offering coherent rebuttals to their plans.

Decentralized Money, the Case for Bitcoin, and Alternate Forms of Currency

Where else do the elites seek to control the populace? By controlling the money supply. One highly effective method for throwing off the shackles of the elites is by refusing to allow governments to force the implementation of CBDC. Cryptocurrencies provide more options for consumers and in a more dynamic marketplace. Because of the anonymity built into the cryptocurrency system, it protects one against state control, providing an option that does quite the opposite of CBDC.[2]

Even before the rise of cryptocurrency, money has been used as a carrot and stick by governments to subjugate a populace. A method of self-sovereignty that citizens have enacted for years is the effort to reduce their taxable income. Investment experts like Robert Kiyosaki have made a career advising people to make their money work for them in his *Rich Dad, Poor Dad* series.[3] One foundational method for doing this is tax-efficient investing in order to reduce the impact taxes have on an individual's assets and better allow their money to grow. Tax-advantaged investing and saving is a tax-efficient strategy for growing wealth and for keeping money.[4]

One thing the pandemic did for people was teach them new ways to get access to things. When certain products like masks, bleach, and toilet paper became scarce, people developed creative ways to gain access to such things.[5] When people found themselves out of work, they found new ways to get what they needed. Bartering briefly made a comeback in 2020 (although it is has since retreated as more people returned to work[6]), and services such as teaching a skill or a musical instrument were traded for products or food; people were meeting their needs by employing methods not used since the Great Depression of the 1930s. Bartering can sometimes grow into sophisticated local networks that include local currencies or community currencies. These alternatives to national currencies necessitate a strong local market and motivated businesses. Some community currencies in the UK, like the Brixton pound and the Totnes Pound, came to prominence during a wave of anti-globalization sentiment.[7] Efforts such as these, in addition to crowdfunding and peer-to-peer (P2P) lending,[8] can strengthen a community and present opportunities to individuals that might otherwise not have been available through traditional lending infrastructure.

These small economic changes make for a very different picture in an ever-changing world. Some tactics like bartering are so old they predate money. Other tools, like cryptocurrency, are still so new we have not yet figured out all the ways they can be employed. But combining these strategies can create a very robust defense mechanism against the methods used by the elites to manipulate money and so create the outcomes they desire. Reducing pressure from taxes, anonymizing transactions, and creating economies among local collectives may help to protect citizens from the coercion inherent in manipulating the money supply.

Natural Medicines

One of the most insidious ways elites control people is via access to healthcare. As more and more health problems are identified, solutions are pumped out. Often the "solutions" to these health issues are woeful at treating the conditions; some do not even treat the problems at all. The example of recent studies on selective serotonin reuptake inhibitors (SSRI) is a good example of this. For decades, the medical industry offered SSRIs as a balm to salve wounded psyches. Doctors regularly diagnosed depression as a chemical imbalance, which they could cure by introducing more serotonin into the brain. In 2022, the medical industry awoke to the reality that this is not true.[9] Proponents of natural solutions and approaches to medicine had been saying so for years, but the alternate approach of more exercise, a better diet and herbal supplements, such as St. John's Wort, were considered reckless and woefully inadequate to righting chemical imbalances in the brain.[10] Warnings from the medical industry ranged from not effective enough, to making the patient sleepy, to having a reaction to other medications. These same reactions, and many others, may occur when taking traditional SSRIs,[11] and herbal remedies can often do a better job of treating certain symptoms. Whilst recommending Vitamin C and D supplementation to treat COVID-19 would have seen you banned from Twitter in 2021 as spreading dangerous, anti-narrative misinformation, those same vitamins have now been shown to have excellent efficacy in fighting coronavirus, especially when taken in liposomal formulations that allow more of the vitamins to be absorbed by the digestive system than traditional tablets or drinks.

The two-decade long explosion of opioid addiction is another dangerous episode in the history of pharmaceutical medicine. Pharmaceutical companies misrepresented the safety and addiction concerns of the drug leading to widespread addiction, crime, and over 500,000 deaths, as the drug became overprescribed at high dosages.[12]

Natural medicines do not have the same track record. Practices like Pranic healing, where the body is given the opportunity to heal itself,[13] and Ayurvedic medicine, where herbal approaches are used,[14] may often solve the problems pharmaceutical medicine might be tempted to address with potent and addictive drugs. Herbal remedies are certainly only a part of a holistic approach to health, but the successes of these remedies, both ancient and recent, offer the view that modern medicine does not necessarily always have the best answers.

Homeschooling

Homeschooling is becoming ever more popular as parents attempt to prevent their children from being indoctrinated. Greater parental control over what children learn, whilst offering them a wider latitude in modern and alternate education subjects, will likely better prepare them for an unknown future where over eighty percent of future jobs probably don't exist today.[15] School systems have long been known to act as tools of the state where children are indoctrinated with notions that are convenient for said state, and where inconvenient narratives are ignored or whitewashed.

Effective ways to sidestep such indoctrination efforts include homeschooling and unschooling children. Homeschooling has, of course, been the subject of various propaganda efforts to rubbish it, but contrary to popular belief, studies have found that homeschooled children are often more successful in the long run, more socially adept than their public-school counterparts, and more independently minded.[16] The "unschooling effort" has created a generation of curious-minded children who are not victimized by school-textbook-sourced propaganda; they are schooled with the values of their parents, who are firmly a part of their education.[17]

Protesting with Your Dollars

One of the most reliable protest methods in economically free societies is voting with dollars. Many people are turning away from predatory tech companies such as Google and Microsoft operating systems to privacy assured alternatives such as Graphene OS, Calyx or Tails OS for example. The fightback begins in your hands or at your desk. A good way to show support for a company, athlete, or an artist whose work is important to a certain ideology, or whose efforts seem heroic, is to support that artist, athlete, or company financially. Conversely, when a media company seems to act in bad faith, a consumer can withhold their money to show distaste. Recently, some media companies have tried to insert certain ideologies into films and have been roundly rejected by consumers. The financial flop of a children's film, *Strange World*, released by Disney, is one such example.[18] Audiences objected to the self-congratulatory tone of the marketing that was centered on the fact the film featured a gay character rather than focusing on trying to make a good movie. Other examples of this pandering and agenda-pushing by huge media companies being rejected by audiences en masse include the children's movie *Lightyear*, the romantic comedy *Bros*, and the thinly veiled political allegory *Amsterdam*.

This principle works the other way as well. For example, when athletes take a political stance they purport to believe in, people who agree with them will support them by purchasing their merchandise. Two examples of this in two drastically different groups are Colin Kaepernick and Ivan Provorov. Regardless of what someone may feel about these two individuals, or the political stands they made, each found overwhelming support from fans who supported these athletes with their money. Colin Kaepernick was a quarterback for the San Francisco 49ers who made headlines in 2017 when he refused to stand for the national anthem, as he felt the need to protest police brutality. He became a firestorm of controversy with some people calling him an opportunist or an ingrate, and others going so far as to boycott or even burn his jersey. However, there were some who found his stance to be brave and genuine and this group flocked to the online merchandise shop to buy his number 7 jersey.[19] In 2023, a hockey player for the Philadelphia Flyers named Ivan Provorov refused to wear a jersey with rainbow-colored numbers on, which the rest of his team was wearing to support the LGBTQA+ community. Provorov refused, citing religious reasons, and while he was called a bigot by many, people who supported his stance spent their money on his jersey to reward him for standing by his principals.[20] These examples reveal that the old adage "money talks" is still true today.

Food Supply

A casual glance through western news stories from the past year reveals a worrying trend in the sudden and often unexplained destruction of the food supply and food processing plants. The modern "just-in-time" logistics of supermarkets exposes the food supply system to fragilities that might not have existed decades earlier. Supermarket supply chains are now so lean that some commentators have remarked (in the UK) that, "we could be only nine meals from anarchy." This is because, on average, most supermarkets only carry enough stock for three days' worth of normal demand. The 2011 UK fuel strikes bore this reality bare as the temporary disruption to fuel deliveries ground the national road-freight logistics network to a near halt. Today's elites know that "an army marches on its stomach." By destroying food supply chains and creating monopoly food firm empires (about eighty percent of the US grocery market share is owned by a few large firms) control is exerted on the population by concentrating the supply of food, one of the basic survival needs highlighted by Maslow. A hungry family is more likely to adhere to state controls in return for the supply of food than go hungry.

Growing food locally and with cooperatives helps to solve this issue, as does severing the reliance on processed fake food, which is predominantly loaded with harmful sugars and other chemicals. Getting in touch with nature again is "food" in two ways: food for the belly and food for the soul. Being outside has proven healing abilities and is often used for the rehabilitation of offenders and the mentally ill. Involving children in the vegetable growing lifecycle offers valuable education in biology and reconnects them with the seasons and nature. Eating seasonally is healthier for you and better for the environment, reducing air miles and distances travelled to stores. Nature provides the right foods for the right season—starchy high carbohydrate vegetables such as turnips and swedes for winter, with lighter fruits and vegetables for when food is abundant in the summer/autumn. Growing organic and low- or no-dig (permaculture) produce offers healthier, more nutrient-packed and higher yielding crops.

Conclusion

To combat the top-down efforts of elites, people must stop transacting in their systems. Individuals should stop watching and reading their propaganda, submitting to their pedagogy, and 9-5 industrial revolution-style work ethic. Local communities must build and empower their own institutions and help each other live a more localized existence, eschewing the negative psychological effects of rampant commercialism and globalization. The elites have constructed a world where it is easy to get access to drugs. Pharmaceuticals have been made cheap, and impediments and protections have been removed. This has made people weak and dependent upon such products. From opioids to cigarettes and alcohol, the ruling class has provided the masses with plenty to dull their wits. It turns out that Marx was wrong when he called religion "the opiate of the masses."[21] It turns out opium is the opiate of the masses.

Furthermore, the ruling class has made cheap credit and misinformation easy to access. Public schooling, with its well-known doctrine of misinforming students, has sent generations of people into the workforce and wider world highly unprepared for the critical thinking necessary to overcome today's conditioning. It is no wonder these same people find themselves deep in debt and wholly reliant on a healthcare system that exploits sickness for profits or is too overburdened to actually solve healthcare issues.[22]

While the societal and medical gains of the past have lifted billions out of poverty, some argue the limits to growth have been reached. For eight billion people to have the same quality of life as an average American, another three globes' worth of natural resources would be required.[23] Rather than the ruling dynasty's solution to population reduction and a return to the Middle Ages' feudal system, we must build a more equitable and spiritual existence. We should strive to return to more natural and homeopathic medicines versus the toxic products produced by big pharma companies, whose business models perpetuate permanent sickness in order to increase profits. The ruling class is powerful and deeply ensconced in the gated communities of thought and control. It will take significant effort to counteract their methods of control. Individual citizens will have to make sacrifices they have never made before and enact the changes that were not conceivable only a few years ago. But these changes are possible. There are methods, tactics, and techniques being developed by local communities, thought leaders, and market disruptors, which can have a drastic impact on the world and systems that seem immutable. Drastically changing the way lives are lived and unseating the powerful is not uncommon. It has happened over and over throughout world history. It is merely a part of how progress is made, of how cycles continue, and how the world changes. From the crossing of the Bering Strait to the French Revolution, from the Great Migration to the October Revolution, the ruling class is always replaced. Nothing lasts forever. The only constant is change.

Throughout it all, it has been the unity of people that has affected change. For better or worse, people are stronger when they are unified. People are stronger when they are working together. There is a common saying that people should "listen to both sides." That is just another talking point of the elite. There are not two sides to any story. That is endless nuance and contradiction. It is just easier for the elite to control the populace if they organize them into two groups and have them face off against one another, instead of contradicting them. Labour Party vs. Conservative Party, Republican vs. Democrat, Manchester vs. Liverpool, Coke vs. Pepsi... there are endless ways people are separated and pitted against one another. Once you transcend these false dichotomies, it is easy to see there is only one humanity, and it is always stronger when it pulls together as one unified group.

Epilogue

It is not uncommon for state agencies to attempt to assert their will on populations secretly, both foreign and domestic. There are many examples of propaganda efforts meant to change people's minds, urge them in certain directions, demonize certain opinions, and reward others. China famously issued Document Number Nine, which called for the destruction of western values.[1]

Considering certain Chinese exports, like TikTok, this puts things into a new and worrying context. Both outlets from the left[2] and the right[3] have warned against the social media app as potential spyware. Not only that, but China has become a very influential demand-side curator of ideas from one of the US's most powerful exports, Hollywood movies. China has influenced US consumers' stances on Taiwan, Chinese technological might, and even cultural issues by holding certain films hostage when they do not conform to Chinese strictures.[4]

Russia has used similar propaganda efforts for decades, albeit their tactics are more intricate and often require long-term efforts to cultivate certain narratives and achieve certain manipulations. Yuri Bezmenov was a KGB spy who revealed a four-step plan for how the former Soviet Union could assert their influence in a country. The first step was a twenty-year program of raising suspicion through academia, journalistic outlets, and even cultural outlets. The second step was about altering a nation economically and defensively. The third step was used many times by the USSR in Central America: when a country had its cultural, economic, and defense systems compromised by multi-year infiltration and propaganda campaigns, they could create a crisis in a matter of weeks. The final phase was normalization, where the changes instituted slowly in the first two steps and quickly in the third step, were made permanent by getting a populace to accept them as normal.[5]

This admission by someone once inside the KGB is chilling, particularly when certain trends are compared to it. Bezmenov talks about the need to recruit not true believers, but narcissists to do the bidding of the KGB, and his approach is apparent when thought leaders like Mark Zuckerberg, Larry Page, and Tim Cook are called out as such.[6]

These propagandistic practices are not unique to China and Russia but bear a striking resemblance to the efforts of western nations. John Perkins' exposé on infiltration and exploitation *Confessions of an Economic Hitman*[7] outlines a similarly shocking short-term and long-term plan for control of a country's decision-making process and its resources.

While countries have long tried to influence the elections, opinions, cultures, and foreign policy decisions of rival nations, it is disturbing when a country like the US or the UK turn those powers of propaganda and control upon their own citizenry as was discovered with the Freedom of Information Act revelations of Operation Roadmap,[8] and in the UK's Investigatory Powers Bill.[9] Many other instances of governments using their vast resources to spy on their own citizens have been revealed and discussed in early chapters of this book, and these are only a small sample of what we know about these governments' capacity for spying, disinformation, and propaganda.

Why does this matter? This matters because it shows that the narrative matters. Information matters. The truth matters so much that governments will spend trillions of dollars to obscure it, manipulate it or distract from it. Yuval Noah Harari, the enfant terrible of the WEF mentioned in chapter four, wrote an entire book about how civilization is nothing more than a narrative. He asks the provocative question, "How do you cause people to believe in an imagined order such as Christianity, democracy, or capitalism? First, you never admit that the order is imagined."[10] His argument is that all of civilization is merely a story. It is a myth that we all believe. He ultimately concludes, "There are no gods, no nations, no money and no human rights, except in our collective imagination."[11]

The narrative is the cornerstone of control. The WEF, the UN, people like Klaus Schwab and Harari, are able to control the world via a convincing story. People like Henry Kissinger are avowed and talented purveyors of compelling fictions. They take a falsehood and then insist upon its veracity. They coerce, cajole and they threaten in order to force people to believe their fiction is the truth. If that does not make the truth compelling, nothing will.

This book has attempted, through its hundreds of citations and its furious adherence to fact, to sort the truth from the fiction. Sometimes, the narratives explored in this book are so fantastical, they have been easy to disprove. Some fictions are more compelling and thus more difficult to disprove. But the attempt has been made to reveal some part of the truth.

The truth matters. It has always mattered. The reason elites try to obscure the truth is because it is so important. It is the truth that will lead us to the actual political, technological, and spiritual evolution that humanity so desperately seeks. We are often so misinformed that we cannot make well-informed decisions. We are so ruined by disinformation that our society has become unjust by default. We cannot grow, improve, or build a healthy society unless we are nourished by the truth.

The quest for truth does not stop on the last page of this book. It is merely the beginning. Good luck on the rest of your awakening journey. Now spread the word!

Notes

Introduction

1. Peele, Jordan, Sean McKittrick, Jason Blum, and Edward H. Hamm. *Get Out*. United States: Universal Pictures, 2017.

2. Essence. "These Black Public Figures Said Yes to the COVID-19 Vaccine." May 3, 2021. https://www.essence.com/news/these-black-celebs-said-yes-to-the-covid-19-vaccine/#1031383

3. Tribune, International Herald. "1964: Attack in the Gulf of Tonkin." *The New York Times*, August 4, 2014. https://archive.nytimes.com/iht-retrospective.blogs.nytimes.com/2014/08/04/1964-attack-in-the-gulf-of-tonkin/

4. Alderson, Andrew; Wavell, Stuart (January 13, 1991). "Paradise lost: The full story of Iraq's violation of Kuwait – Gulf Crisis". Sunday Times.

5. "Experts: Iraq Has Tons of Chemical Weapons." CNN. Cable News Network. Accessed January 27, 2023. https://www.cnn.com/2002/WORLD/meast/09/02/iraq.weapons/index.html

6. Gordon, Michael R., and Judith Miller. "US Says Hussein Intensifies Quest for A-BOMB Parts." *The New York Times*, September 8, 2002. https://www.nytimes.com/2002/09/08/world/threats-responses-iraqis-us-says-hussein-intensifies-quest-for-bomb-parts.html

7. "Blair: Why Saddam and His Weapons Have to Be Stopped." The Guardian. Guardian News and Media, September 25, 2002. https://www.theguardian.com/politics/2002/sep/25/uk.iraq

8. Paterson, Pat. "The Truth about Tonkin." US Naval Institute, September 22, 2022. https://www.usni.org/magazines/naval-history-magazine/2008/february/truth-about-tonkin

9. Leonard Doyle, "Iraqi Baby Atrocity is Revealed as Myth," The Independent (12 January 1992) p. 11.

10. Comey, James. *A Higher Loyalty: Truth, Lies, and Leadership.* St Martins Pr, 2018.

11. Peter Castagno, Citizen Truth December 11. "Pelosi Knew Bush Lied about Iraq but Didn't Consider It Impeachable." Citizen Truth, December 11, 2019. https://citizentruth.org/pelosi-knew-bush-lied-about-iraq-but-didnt-consider-it-impeachable/

12. O'Neill, Tom, and Dan Piepenbring. "Inside the Archive of an LSD Researcher with Ties to the CIA's Mkultra Mind Control Project." The Intercept. The Intercept, November 24, 2019. https://theintercept.com/2019/11/24/cia-mkultra-louis-jolyon-west/

13. Hearn, Kelly. "The Rise of Unregulated Drug Trials in South America." The Nation, June 29, 2015. https://www.thenation.com/article/archive/rise-unregulated-drug-trials-south-america/

14. "Tuskegee Study - Timeline - Cdc - Os." Centers for Disease Control and Prevention. December 5, 2022. https://www.cdc.gov/tuskegee/timeline.htm

15. Washington, Harriet (October 1994). "Henrietta Lacks: An Unsung Hero". *Emerge Magazine.*

16. Gross, Terry. "The CIA's Secret Quest for Mind Control: Torture, LSD and a 'Poisoner in Chief'." NPR. September 9, 2019. https://www.npr.org/2019/09/09/758989641/the-cias-secret-quest-for-mind-control-torture-lsd-and-a-poisoner-in-chief

17. Schumm, Laura. "What Was Operation Paperclip?" History.com. A&E Television Networks, June 2, 2014. https://www.history.com/news/what-was-operation-paperclip

18. Little, Becky. "Why Martin Luther King's Family Believes James Earl Ray Was Not His Killer." History.com. A&E Television Networks, April 4, 2018. https://www.history.com/news/who-killed-martin-luther-king-james-earl-ray-mlk-assassination

19. History.com Editors. "Iran-Contra Affair." History.com. A&E Television Networks, August 10, 2017. https://www.history.com/topics/1980s/iran-contra-affair

20. Katz, Jonathan M. "The Plot against American Democracy That

Isn't Taught in Schools." Rolling Stone. Rolling Stone, January 1, 2022. https://www.rollingstone.com/politics/politics-features/coup-jan6-fdr-new-deal-business-plot-1276709/

21. "Libor Scandal: The Bankers Who Fixed the World's Most Important Number | Liam Vaughan and Gavin Finch." The Guardian. Guardian News and Media, January 18, 2017. https://www.theguardian.com/business/2017/jan/18/libor-scandal-the-bankers-who-fixed-the-worlds-most-important-number

22. History.com Editors. "Watergate Scandal." History.com. A&E Television Networks, October 29, 2009. https://www.history.com/topics/1970s/watergate

23. "Edward Snowden: How the Spy Story of the Age Leaked Out." The Guardian. Guardian News and Media, June 12, 2013. https://www.theguardian.com/world/2013/jun/11/edward-snowden-nsa-whistleblower-profile

Chapter 1: Has There Ever Been True Democracy?

1. Hancock, Graham. *Fingerprints of the Gods: The Evidence of Earth's Lost Civilization*. Crown Publishing Group, 1995.

2. Vigato, Marco M. *The Empires of Atlantis: The Origins of Ancient Civilizations and Mystery Traditions throughout the Ages*. Bear & Company, 2022.

3. History.com Editors. 2018. "Hunter Gatherers." HISTORY. A&E Television Networks. August 21, 2018.

4. Savoia, Antonio, Joshy Easaw, and Andrew McKay. 2010. "Inequality, Democracy, and Institutions: A Critical Review of Recent Research." World Development 38 (2): 142–54.

5. Sadowski, Ryszard F. 2017. "Neolithic Revolution." Encyclopedia of Food and Agricultural Ethics, 1–8. https://doi.org/10.10 07/978-94-007-6167-4_540-1

6. Flax, Matthew. 2022. "Neolithic Revolution: A Turning Point in Human History." Owlcation. November 4, 2022. https://owlca tion.com/humanities/neolithic-revolution

7. Lanchester, John. 2017. "How Civilization Started." *The New Yorker*. September 11, 2017. https://www.newyorker.com/mag azine/2017/09/18/the-case-against-civilization

8. Dyble, Mark, Jack Thorley, Abigail E. Page, Daniel Smith, and Andrea Bamberg Migliano. 2019. "Engagement in Agricultural Work Is Associated with Reduced Leisure Time among Agta Hunter-Gatherers." Nature Human Behaviour 3 (8): 792–96. https://doi.org/10.1038/s41562-019-0614-6

9. Flax, Matthew. 2022. "Neolithic Revolution: A Turning Point in Human History." Owlcation. November 4, 2022. https://owlca tion.com/humanities/neolithic-revolution

10. Kohler, Timothy A., Michael E. Smith, Amy Bogaard, Gary M. Feinman, Christian E. Peterson, Alleen Betzenhauser, Matthew Pailes, et al. 2017. "Greater Post-Neolithic Wealth Disparities in Eurasia than in North America and Mesoamerica." Nature 551 (7682): 619–22. https://doi.org/10.1038/nature2464

11. Fochesato, Mattia and Samuel Bowles. 2017. "Technology, Institutions, and Wealth Inequality over Eleven Millennia | Santa Fe Institute." Www.santafe.edu 2017. https://www.santafe.edu/research/results/working-papers/technology-institutions-and-wealth-inequality-over

12. "Prehistory: Power and Politics." English Heritage. Accessed January 28, 2023. https://www.english-heritage.org.uk/learn/story-of-england/prehistory/power-and-politics/

13. Eaton, Victor. "7 Oldest Governments in the World." Oldest.org, May 11, 2022. https://www.oldest.org/politics/governments/#:~:text=7%2520 Oldest%2520Governments%2520in%2520the%2520World%2520 01%25201.,%25E2%2580%2593%25201453%2520CE%2520... %25207%25207.%2520Japan%2520

14. Author Carrie Golus. "Five Things I Learned about Sumerian Beer." The University of Chicago Magazine. Accessed January 28, 2023. https://mag.uchicago.edu/arts-humanities/five-things-i-learned-about-sumerian-beer

15. "Bria 20 2 C Hobbes, Locke, Montesquieu, and Rousseau on Government." Constitutional Rights Foundation. Accessed January 28, 2023. https://www.crf-usa.org/bill-of-rights-in-action/bria-20-2-c-hobbes-locke-montesquieu-and-rousseau-on-government.html

16. Bogdanor, Vernon. "The Evolution of Constitutional Monarchy." The Monarchy and the Constitution, 1997, 1–41. https:

//doi.org/10.1093/0198293348.003.0001

17. "Constitutional Monarchy." Encyclopædia Britannica. Encyclopædia Britannica, inc. Accessed January 28, 2023. https://www.britannica.com/topic/constitutional-monarchy

18. Branthoover, Sam. "Divine Monarchy: Exploitative or Beneficial? Sam Branthoover." Mises Institute, August 8, 2022. https://mises.org/library/divine-monarchy-exploitative-or-beneficial

19. Hoppe, Hans-Hermann. "From Aristocracy to Monarchy to Democracy." Mises Institute. Accessed January 28, 2023. https://cdn.mises.org/From%20Aristocracy%20to%20Monarchy%20to%20Democracy_Hoppe_Text%202014.pdf

20. Hoppe, Hans-Hermann. "From Aristocracy to Monarchy to Democracy." Mises Institute. (pp. 62-63) Accessed January 28, 2023. https://cdn.mises.org/From%20Aristocracy%20to%20Monarchy%20to%20Democracy_Hoppe_Text%202014.pdf

21. "From Aristocracy to Monarchy to Democracy Audiobook: Hans-Hermann Hoppe." Mises Institute, February 17, 2015. https://mises.org/library/aristocracy-monarchy-democracy-audiobook

Chapter 2: The Great "United Nations"-Reset

1. *Solaris* by Stanislaw Lem (2016). Faber and Faber

2. "Batman." Directed by Leslie H. Martinson, performances by Adam West, Burt Ward, and Cesar Romero, 20th Century Fox,

1966.

3. "Live and Let Die." Directed by Guy Hamilton, performances by Roger Moore, Yaphet Kotto, and Jane Seymour, Eon Productions, 1973.

4. "Captain America: Civil War." Directed by Anthony and Joe Russo, performances by Chris Evans, Robert Downey Jr., and Sebastian Stan, Marvel Studios, 2016.

5. "Vision Statement | General Assembly of the United Nations." United Nations. United Nations. Accessed January 28, 2023. https://www.un.org/pga/74/documents/vision-statement/

6. "Hotel Rwanda." Directed by Terry George, performances by Don Cheadle, Sophie Okonedo, and Joaquin Phoenix, United Artists, 2004.

7. The Nixon Administration and the United Nations: "It's a Damned Debating Society" Dr. Edward C. Keefer

8. "Q&A: Oil-for-food scandal". BBC News. 7 September 2005. Archived from the original on 3 December 2013. Retrieved 27 November 2013. http://news.bbc.co.uk/2/hi/middle_east/4131602.stm

9. "UN admits Sri Lanka civil war failure." Bangkok Post, August 8, 2005. Retrieved from https://www.bangkokpost.com/world/321218/un-admits-sri-lanka-civil-war-failure accessed January 28, 2023.

10. Shea, Jamie. "1967: De Gaulle pulls France out of NATO's inte-

grated military structure." 12 December 2016. https://www.nat o.int/cps/en/natohq/opinions_139272.htm

11. Sneha Barot Susan A. Cohen, Sneha Barot, and Susan A. Co-hen. "The Global Gag Rule and Fights over Funding UNFPA: The Issues That Won't Go Away." Guttmacher Institute, August 30, 2022. https://www.guttmacher.org/gpr/2015/06/global-ga g-rule-and-fights-over-funding-unfpa-issues-wont-go-away

12. "The Nixon Administration and the United Nations: 'It's a Damned Debating Society'", Archived 26 November 2007 at the Wayback Machine, Dr. Edward C. Keefer (PDF).

13. "Agenda 21." United Nations, 1992. https://www.un.org/esa/d sd/agenda21/res_agenda21_00.shtml

14. "Agenda 21: Sustainable Development Knowledge Platform." United Nations. Accessed January 28, 2023. https://sustainabl edevelopment.un.org/outcomedocuments/agenda21

15. PMF IAS. "Earth Summit 1992, UN Environment, Rio+20, CBD, UNFCCC." PMF IAS, June 11, 2019. https://www.pmf ias.com/earth-summit-unced-unfccc/

16. "Sustainable Development Goals: 17 Goals to Transform Our World." United Nations. United Nations. Accessed January 28, 2023. https://www.un.org/en/exhibits/page/sdgs-17-goals-trans form-world

17. The Political Impact of the Sustainable Development Goals Transforming Governance Through Global Goals? p. 59 – 91,

DOI: https://doi.org/10.1017/9781009082945.004, Publisher: Cambridge University Press, Print publication year: 2022

18. "G20 Bali Leaders' Declaration." The White House. The United States Government, November 16, 2022. https://www.whitehouse.gov/briefing-room/statements-releases/2022/11/16/g20-bali-leaders-declaration/

19. "UN Environment Document Repository Home." Accessed January 28, 2023. https://wedocs.unep.org/bitstream/handle/20.500.11822/35875/K2100501-e.pdf

20. "2050 Archives - United Nations Sustainable Development." United Nations. Accessed January 28, 2023. https://www.un.org/sustainabledevelopment/blog/tag/2050/

21. Federal Office for Spatial Development ARE. "1987: Brundtland Report." Bundesamt Raumentwicklung ARE. Accessed January 28, 2023. https://www.are.admin.ch/are/en/home/media/publications/sustainable-development/brundtland-report.html

22. Gomez, Christian. *Exposing The 2030 Agenda*. 2022. Exposing-2030-Agenda-Booklet.pdf (jbs.org)

23. THE LIMITS TO GROWTH: A REPORT FOR THE CLUB OF ROME'S PROJECT ON THE PREDICAMENT OF MANKIND Donella H. Meadows Dennis L. Meadows Jorgen Randers William W. Behrens III

24. King, Alexander, and Bertrand Schneider. *The First Global Revolution: A Report by the Council of the Club of Rome*. New York:

Pantheon Books, 1991., p.75

25. Designing a Brave New World: Eugenics, Politics, and Fiction, JOANNE WOIAK, The Public Historian, Vol. 29, No. 3 (Summer 2007), pp. 105-129 (25 pages), Published By: University of California Press

26. Ehret, Matthew. "The Rise of the 'Predictive Modelling' Mafia." Unlimited Hangout, November 22, 2022. https://unlimitedhangout.com/2022/11/investigative-reports/the-club-of-rome-and-the-rise-of-the-predictive-modelling-mafia/

27. Ehret, Matthew. "The Rise of the 'Predictive Modelling' Mafia." Unlimited Hangout, November 22, 2022. https://unlimitedhangout.com/2022/11/investigative-reports/the-club-of-rome-and-the-rise-of-the-predictive-modelling-mafia/

28. Presse, AFP - Agence France. "'We Need a Single Global Order' Says Macron at APEC Summit." Barron's. Barrons, November 18, 2022. https://www.barrons.com/news/we-need-a-single-global-order-says-macron-at-apec-summit-01668779420

29. "Address Before a Joint Session of the Congress on the Persian Gulf Crisis and the Federal Budget Deficit." The American Presidency Project, September 11, 1990. https://www.presidency.ucsb.edu/documents/address-before-joint-session-the-congress-the-persian-gulf-crisis-and-the-federal-budget

30. Friedman, Milton, and P. N. Snowden. 2002. *Capitalism and Freedom*. Chicago, IL: University of Chicago Press.

31. Buchanan, Patrick J. "Kissinger Calls for a New World Order: Buchanan." Asbury Park Press. Asbury Park Press, April 8, 2020. https://www.app.com/story/opinion/columnists/2020/0 4/08/henry-kissinger-calls-new-world-order/2961577001/

32. A. Grice, "This was the Bretton Woods of our times: Mr. Brown deserves credit. He played a blinder at the summit," The Independent, Apr. 2009.

Chapter 3: The Road to Davos

1. Ceri Parker Previously Commissioning Editor, and Ceri Parker. "Davos at 50: A Timeline of Highlights." WEF. Accessed January 28, 2023. https://www.weforum.org/agenda/2019/12/world-ec onomic-forum-davos-at-50-history-a-timeline-of-highlights/

2. Mann, Thomas. *The Magic Mountain*. London: Woolf Haus, 1924.

3. ABC News. "What Is Davos and Why Are so Many Important People Talking about It?" ABC News. ABC News, January 22, 2020. https://www.abc.net.au/news/2020-01-22/davos-world-e conomic-forum-meeting-explained/11888724

4. Zimonjic, Peter. "WEF Official Says Canada Has Bigger Issues to Discuss than Conspiracy Theories | CBC News." CBCnews. CBC/Radio Canada, September 3, 2022. https://www.cbc.ca/news/politics/adrian-monck-world-e

conomic-forum-house-interview-1.6571569

5. "The Magic Meeting Place: Europe's Corporate Chiefs Go to Davos for Play and Work." Time. Time Inc., February 16, 1981. https://content.time.com/time/subscriber/article/0,3300 9,954677,00.html

6. Schreiber, Markus. "Klaus Schwab on the History of the WEF, Greta Thunberg and Trump." World Today News, January 20, 2020. https://www.world-today-news.com/klaus-schwab-on-th e-history-of-the-wef-greta-thunberg-and-trump/

7. Harvard Programs Received CIA Help, *The New York Times*, April 16th, 1967

8. "Profile of William Yandell Elliot." Executive Intelligence Review, vol. 29, no. 3, January 25, 2002. William Yandell Elliott (larouch epub.com)

9. The WEF A Partner in Shaping History: The First 40 Years 1971 – 2010. https://www3.weforum.org/docs/WEF_First40Years_Bo ok_2010.pdf

10. Menand, Louis. "Fat Man." *The New Yorker*, June 20, 2005. htt ps://www.newyorker.com/magazine/2005/06/27/fat-man

11. Henderson, David. "Henderson's Criticisms and Appreciations of John Kenneth Galbraith." Econlib, April 19, 2022. https://www.econlib.org/hendersons-criticisms-and-appr eciations-of-john-kenneth-galbraith/

12. Meaney, Thomas. "The Myth of Henry Kissinger." The New

Yorker, May 11, 2020. https://www.newyorker.com/magazine/
2020/05/18/the-myth-of-henry-kissinger

13. Vedmore, Johnny. "Dr. Klaus Schwab or: How the CFR Taught
Me to Stop Worrying and Love the Bomb." VK. VK, March 13,
2022. https://vk.com/@secretxgovernment-dr-klaus-schwab-or
-how-the-cfr-taught-me-to-stop-worrying-an

14. Vedmore, Johnny. "Dr. Klaus Schwab or: How the CFR Taught
Me to Stop Worrying and Love the Bomb." VK. VK, March 13,
2022. https://vk.com/@secretxgovernment-dr-klaus-schwab-or
-how-the-cfr-taught-me-to-stop-worrying-an

15. "Young Global Leaders." Young Global Leaders. Accessed January 28, 2023. https://www.influencewatch.org/organization/yo
ung-global-leaders/

16. Wauters, Robin. "WEF Announces New Batch of Young Global
Leaders (Mark Zuckerberg, Chad Hurley, Kevin Rose and
More)." TechCrunch, February 25, 2009.
https://techcrunch.com/2009/02/25/world-economic-forum-a
nnounces-new-batch-of-young-global-leaders-mark-zuckerberg
-chad-hurley-kevin-rose-and-more/

17. skellycat9. "Klaus Schwab/Harvard Talk/ Trudeau Cabinet &
Others 'Penetrated'." YouTube. YouTube, January 26, 2022. h
ttps://www.youtube.com/watch?v=b4cDNyvrP40

18. Corcoran, Terence. "In Canada, Follow the Money + The Ideas."
Financial Post, February 18, 2022. https://financialpost.com/op
inion/terence-corcoran-in-canada-follow-the-money-the-ideas

19. Nordangard, Jacob. "WEF's 'Young Global Leaders' Revealed." Global Research, January 21, 2023. https://www.globalresearch.ca/world-economic-forum-young-global-leaders-revealed/5769766

20. Vedmore, Johnny. "The Unauthorized History of the WEF's Young Global Leaders Program." Unlimited Hangout, December 8, 2022. https://unlimitedhangout.com/2022/08/investigative-reports/the-kissinger-continuum-the-unauthorized-history-of-the-wefs-young-global-leaders-program/

21. Ramaswamy, Vivek. "'Stakeholder Capitalism' Review: The Global, Olympian 'We'." The Wall Street Journal. Dow Jones & Company, January 25, 2021. https://www.wsj.com/articles/stakeholder-capitalism-review-the-global-olympian-we-11611614435

22. D'Souza, Deborah. "What Is Stakeholder Capitalism?" Investopedia. Investopedia, December 19, 2022. https://www.investopedia.com/stakeholder-capitalism-4774323

23. Denning, Steve. "Why Stakeholder Capitalism Will Fail." Forbes. Forbes Magazine, October 12, 2022. https://www.forbes.com/sites/stevedenning/2020/01/05/why-stakeholder-capitalism-will-fail/?sh=65cccd4f785a

24. Engdahl, F. William. "Dangerous Alliance of Rothschild and Vatican of Francis." New Age | The Most Popular Outspoken English Daily in Bangladesh. Accessed January 28,

2023. https://www.newagebd.net/article/125494/dangerous-al
liance-of-rothschild-and-vatican-of-francis

25. Staff, Fortune. "Big Companies Join Vatican-Affiliated Council Pledging Inclusive Capitalism." Fortune. Fortune, December 8, 2020. https://fortune.com/2020/12/08/council-for-inclusive-c apitalism-with-the-vatican/

26. "Stakeholder Capitalism and ESG-the Road to Socialism: Op-Ed." Fraser Institute, January 21, 2022. https://www.fraserinstitute.org/article/stakeholder-capit alism-and-esg-the-road-to-socialism

27. Chumley, Cheryl K. "Stakeholder Capitalism Is Communism in Disguise." The Washington Times. The Washington Times, September 28, 2021. https://www.washingtontimes.com/news/202 1/sep/28/stakeholder-capitalism-communism-disguise/

28. Haskins, Justin, and Jack McPherrin. "The Heartland Institute." – The Heartland Institute. Accessed January 28, 2023. https://www.heartland.org/publications-resources/publications /understanding-environmental-social-and-governance-esg-metri cs-a-basic-primer

29. Schwab, Klaus; Malleret, Thierry (2020). *COVID-19: The Great Reset (1 ed.).* Cologny/Geneva Schweiz: Forum Publishing. ISBN 9782940631124. OCLC 1193302829. Amazon.com: COVID-19: The Great Reset: 9782940631124: Schwab, Klaus, Malleret, Thierry: Books

30. Schwab, Klaus; Malleret, Thierry (2020). *COVID-19: The*

Great Reset (1 ed.). Cologny/Geneva Schweiz: Forum Publishing. ISBN 9782940631124. OCLC 1193302829. Amazon.com: COVID-19: The Great Reset: 9782940631124: Schwab, Klaus, Malleret, Thierry: Books

31. Carmichael, Flora, and Jack Goodman. "The Coronavirus Pandemic 'Great Reset' Theory and a False Vaccine Claim Debunked." BBC News. BBC, November 22, 2020. https://www.bbc.com/news/55017002

32. "Now Is the Time for a 'Great Reset'." WEF. Accessed January 28, 2023. https://www.weforum.org/agenda/2020/06/now-is-the-time-for-a-great-reset/

33. Aure. "I Read Klaus Schwab's 'The Great Reset' so You Don't Have To." Medium. Books Are Our Superpower, September 27, 2021. https://baos.pub/i-read-klaus-schwabs-the-great-reset-so-you-don-t-have-to-e335416a1feb

34. Whiting, Kate, Maxwell Hall, Penny Abeywardena, Global Citizen, Sebastian Troëng, Cesar Augusto Mba Abogo, Brian A. Wong, Sarah Kirby, et al. "The Great Reset." WEF. Accessed January 28, 2023. https://www.weforum.org/focus/the-great-reset

35. Meadows, Donella H., Dennis L. Meadows, Jørgen Randers, and William W. Behrens. "Donella Meadows Collection." The Limits to Growth: A report for the Club of Rome's project on the predicament of mankind. Accessed January 28, 2023. https://collections.dartmouth.edu/teitexts/meadows/diplomatic/meadows_ltg-diplomatic.html

36. Betz, Bradford. "WEF Chair Klaus Schwab Declares on Chinese State TV: 'China Is a Model for Many Nations'." MSN, November 23, 2022. https://www.msn.com/en-us/news/world/world-economic-forum-chair-klaus-schwab-declares-on-chinese-state-tv-china-is-a-model-for-many-nations/ar-AA14tRvy?li=BBnb7Kz

37. "In Conversation with Henry Kissinger." WEF. Accessed January 28, 2023. https://www.weforum.org/agenda/2022/05/kissinger-these-are-the-main-geopolitical-challenges-facing-the-world-right-now/

38. Aure. "I Read Klaus Schwab's 'The Great Reset' so You Don't Have To." Medium. Books Are Our Superpower, September 27, 2021. https://baos.pub/i-read-klaus-schwabs-the-great-reset-so-you-don-t-have-to-e335416a1feb

Chapter 4: The (not so) Great Reset

1. Pomeroy, Robin. "The Great Reset - A Blueprint for a Better World after Covid." WEF, June 4, 2020. https://www.weforum.org/agenda/2020/06/the-great-reset-this-weeks-world-vs-virus-podcast/

2. World Economic Forum. "Special Address by H.R.H.. the Prince of Wales | Davos 2020." YouTube, January 22, 2020. https://www.youtube.com/watch?v=W9OLNQULa1I

3. Wecke, Ivan. "Conspiracy Theories aside, There Is Something Fishy about the Great Reset." openDemocracy, August 16,

2021. https://www.opendemocracy.net/en/oureconomy/conspiracy-theories-aside-there-something-fishy-about-great-reset/

4. Curated Alternative Narratives. "Meet Yuval Noah Harari, the Prophet of the World's Ruling Class - What He Thinks and What He Believes Is Coming." The Rio Times, September 1, 2022. https://www.riotimesonline.com/brazil-news/modern-day-censorship/meet-yuval-noah-harari-the-messiah-of-the-worlds-ruling-class-what-he-thinks-and-what-he-believes-is-coming/

5. Harari, Yuval Noah. *Sapiens: A Brief History of Humankind*. New York: Harper, 2014. Print.

6. Bloom, Howard K. *The Lucifer Principle: A Scientific Expedition into the Forces of History*. New York: Atlantic Monthly Press, 1997.

7. Greene, Brian. *The Elegant Universe*. London: Vintage Digital, 2011.

8. Harari, Yuval Noah. *Sapiens: A Brief History of Humankind*. New York: Harper, 2014. Print. Chapter 11

9. Harari, Yuval Noah. "Are Humans Becoming More God-like?" GE News, November 15, 2015. https://www.ge.com/news/reports/are-humans-becoming-more-god-like-interview-with-yuval-noah-harari-of-hebrew-university

10. Narayanan, Darshana. "The Dangerous Populist Science of Yuval Noah Harari - Current Affairs." Current Affairs. Accessed Febru-

ary 1, 2023. https://www.currentaffairs.org/2022/07/the-dange
rous-populist-science-of-yuval-noah-harari

11. Hallpike, C. R. "A Response to Yuval Harari's 'Sapiens: A Brief History of Humankind'." New English Review. Accessed February 1, 2023. https://www.newenglishreview.org/articles/a-respo
nse-to-yuval-hararis-sapiens-a-brief-history-of-humankind/

12. Chollet, François. "The Last Kind Is Cognitive Autonomy: Creating Artificial Minds That Could Thrive Independently of Us, That Would Exist for Their Own Sake. Today and for the Foreseeable Future, This Is Stuff of Science Fiction." Twitter, March 19, 2021. https://twitter.com/fchollet/status/13730318111487
71331

13. Harari, Yuval N. *Homo Deus: A Brief History of Tomorrow*. Amazon.   Harper   Perennial,   2018. https://www.amazon.com/Homo-Deus-Brief-History-Tomorro
w/dp/0062464345/ref=pd_lpo_1?pd_rd_w=ALVPK&content
-id=amzn1.sym.116f529c-aa4d-4763-b2b6-4d614ec7dc00&pf_
rd_p=116f529c-aa4d-4763-b2b6-4d614ec7dc00&pf_rd_r=YY
VMBTH8H09YW54WD97Q&pd_rd_wg=KWTx3&pd_rd_r
=af64377f-cd76-4d88-aadd-e6119bd30d0a&pd_rd_i=0062464
345&psc=1

14. Kelley, David. "What Is Objectivism?, The Atlas Society: Ayn Rand, Objectivism, Atlas Shrugged." The Atlas Society | Ayn Rand, Objectivism, Atlas Shrugged, June 14, 2010. https://ww
w.atlassociety.org/post/what-is-objectivism

15.

Garfinkel, Avi. "Yuval Noah Harari's Dangerous New Morality." Haaretz.com. Haaretz, December 16, 2022. https://www.haaretz.com/israel-news/2022-12-16/ty-article/.highlight/yuval-noah-hararis-dangerous-new-morality/00000185-1ba7-dfc4-aff7-fbbf8f2d0000

16. Schwab, Klaus. "The Fourth Industrial Revolution: What It Means and How to Respond." WEF, January 14, 2016. https://www.weforum.org/agenda/2016/01/the-fourth-industrial-revolution-what-it-means-and-how-to-respond/

17. "Regulation for the Fourth Industrial Revolution." GOV.UK. Accessed February 1, 2023. https://www.gov.uk/government/publications/regulation-for-the-fourth-industrial-revolution/regulation-for-the-fourth-industrial-revolution

18. Department for Digital, Culture, Media & Sport. "Matt Hancock's Speech in Davos on Reimagining Policy-Making for the Fourth Industrial Revolution." GOV.UK, January 25, 2018. https://www.gov.uk/government/speeches/reimagining-policy-making-for-4ir-closing-speech

19. Department for Digital, Culture, Media & Sport. "The Fourth Industrial Revolution." GOV.UK, October 16, 2017. https://www.gov.uk/government/speeches/the-4th-industrial-revolution

20. Morgan, Jamie. "The Fourth Industrial Revolution Could Lead to a Dark Future." The Conversation, January 9, 2020. https://theconversation.com/the-fourth-industrial-revol

ution-could-lead-to-a-dark-future-125897

21. Sikh for Truth. "Sinister Aims of the WEF's Fourth Industrial Revolution (Great Reset) Exposed." The Expose, November
22, 2022. https://expose-news.com/2022/11/23/wef-sinister-gr
eat-reset-exposed/

22. Harari, Yuval Noah. "Yuval Noah Harari: The World after Coronavirus: Free to Read." Financial Times, March 20, 2020. https:/
/www.ft.com/content/19d90308-6858-11ea-a3c9-1fe6fedcca75

23. Harari, Yuval Noah. "Yuval Noah Harari: The World after Coronavirus: Free to Read." Financial Times, March 20, 2020. https:/
/www.ft.com/content/19d90308-6858-11ea-a3c9-1fe6fedcca75

24. Gleckman, Harris. "How the United Nations Is Quietly Being
Turned into a Public-Private Partnership." openDemocracy, July
2,   2019.
https://www.opendemocracy.net/en/oureconomy/how-united
-nations-quietly-being-turned-public-private-partnership/?sourc
e=in-article-related-story

25. "G20 Bali Leaders' Declaration 2022, Bali, 15-16 November
2022." Accessed February 2, 2023. https://www.consilium.euro
pa.eu/media/60201/2022-11-16-g20-declaration-data.pdf

26. Staff of the IMF. "G-20 2020 Report on Strong, Sustainable,
Balanced, and Inclusive Growth." IMF, November 1, 2020. ht
tps://www.imf.org/external/np/g20/110220.htm

27. Norton, Tom. "Fact Check: Were Bill Gates and WEF's

Klaus Schwab at G20 This Year?" Newsweek, November 17, 2022. https://www.newsweek.com/were-bill-gates-world-econo mic-forum-klaus-schwab-g20-this-year-1760386

28. Gosling, Tony. "Bill Gates Buying Farmland, Welcome to Neo-Feudalism: A Closer Look at Farmer Bill." The Land Is Ours, July 12, 2022. https://tlio.org.uk/bill-gates-buying-farmland-w elcome-to-neo-feudalism-a-closer-look-at-farmer-bill/

Chapter 5: Pandemic or Scamdemic? Part 1

1. Dolgin, Elie. "The tangled history of mRNA vaccines." Nature News. Nature Publishing Group, September 14, 2021. https:// www.nature.com/articles/d41586-021-02483-w

2. "How Vaccines Are Made, and Why It Is Hard." The Economist. The Economist Newspaper. Accessed February 1, 2023. https://www.economist.com/science-and-technology/20 21/02/06/how-vaccines-are-made-and-why-it-is-hard

3. Demasi, Maryanne. "FDA Oversight of Clinical Trials Is 'Grossly Inadequate,'" Say Experts." The BMJ. British Medical Journal Publishing Group, November 16, 2022. https://www.bmj.com /content/379/bmj.o2628

4. Radcliffe, Shawn. "FDA Oversight of Clin- ical Trials Was 'Grossly Inadequate,' Report Claims." Healthline. Healthline Media, November 18, 2022. https://www.healthline.com/health-news/fda-oversight -of-clinical-trials-was-grossly-inadequate-report-claims

5. Wallace-Wells, David. "We Had the Vaccine the Whole Time." Intelligencer, December 7, 2020. https://nymag.com/intelligencer/2020/12/moderna-covid-19-vaccine-design.html

6. Chossudovsky, Michel. "The Who Confirms That the COVID-19 PCR Test Is Flawed." SOTN: Alternative News, Analysis & Commentary, August 11, 2021. https://stateofthenation.co/?p=78557

7. "Who Information Notice for Users 2020/05." World Health Organization, January 13, 2021. https://www.who.int/news/item/20-01-2021-who-information-notice-for-ivd-users-2020-05

8. "Who Information Notice for Users 2020/05." World Health Organization. World Health Organization, January 13, 2021. https://www.who.int/news/item/20-01-2021-who-information-notice-for-ivd-users-2020-05

9. Dupuy, Beatrice. "Who Did Not Say PCR Test Flaw Led to Overstated COVID-19 Cases." AP NEWS. Associated Press, January 28, 2021. https://apnews.com/article/fact-checking-9913596351

10. Gallagher, James. "Are Coronavirus Tests Flawed?" BBC News. BBC, February 13, 2020. https://www.bbc.com/news/health-51491763

11. "Lab Alert: Changes to CDC RT-PCR for SARS-COV-2 Testing (Cdc.gov)." Centers for Disease Control and Prevention, January 27, 2023. https://www.cdc.gov/locs/2021/07-21-2021-lab-alert-Changes_CDC_RT-PCR_SARS-CoV-2_Testing_1.html

12. Chossudovsky, Michel. *The Worldwide Corona Crisis: Global Coup d'État Against Humanity: Destroying Civil Society, Engineered Economic Depression*. Global Research Publishers, Centre for Research on Globalization (CRG), 2022.

13. NIAID. "Anthony S. Fauci, M.D." National Institute of Allergy and Infectious Diseases. US Department of Health and Human Services. Accessed February 1, 2023. https://www.niaid.nih.gov /about/Anthony-s-fauci-md-bio

14. Kennedy, Robert Francis. *The Real Anthony Fauci: Bill Gates, Big Pharma, and the Global War on Democracy and Public Health*. New York: Skyhorse Publishing, 2022.

15. Broderick, Ryan. "Trump's Biggest Supporters Think the Coronavirus Is a Deep State Plot." BuzzFeed News. BuzzFeed News, July 6, 2020. https://www.buzzfeednews.com/article/ryanhates this/trump-supporters-coronavirus-deep-state-qanon

16. Davidson, Helen. "Global Report: Virus Has Unleashed a 'Tsunami of Hate' across World, Says UN Chief." The Guardian. Guardian News and Media, May 8, 2020. https://www.theguardian.com/world/2020/may/08/global-rep ort-china-open-to-cooperate-with-who-on-virus-origin-as-trum p-repeats-lab-claim

17. Rutz, David. "New York Times Health Reporter: Wuhan Lab Leak Coronavirus Theory Has 'Racist Roots,' Isn't 'Plausible'." Fox News. FOX News Network, May 26, 2021. https://www.foxnews.com/media/new-york-times-health-report

er-wuhan-lab-leak-coronavirus-theory-has-racist-roots-isnt-plaus
ible

18. Rutz, David. "CNN Medical Contributor: Don't Let
    Lab-Leak Theory Lead to Anti-Asian Discrimina-
    tion." Fox News. FOX News Network, June 2,
    2021. https://www.foxnews.com/media/cnn-medical-contribut
    or-dont-let-lab-leak-theory-lead-to-anti-asian-discrimination

19. Mecklin, John. "The Origin of COVID: Did People or Nature
    Open Pandora's Box at Wuhan?" Bulletin of the Atomic
    Scientists,   July   1,   2022.
    https://thebulletin.org/2021/05/the-origin-of-covid-did-people
    -or-nature-open-pandoras-box-at-wuhan/?utm_source=Twitter
    &utm_medium=SocialMedia&utm_campaign=TwitterPost052
    021&utm_content=DisruptiveTechnologies_OriginCovid_050
    52021

20. Kessler, Glenn. "Analysis | Timeline: How the Wuhan Lab-Leak
    Theory Suddenly Became Credible." The Washington Post. WP
    Company,   May   27,   2021.
    https://www.washingtonpost.com/politics/2021/05/25/timelin
    e-how-wuhan-lab-leak-theory-suddenly-became-credible/

21. Latham, Jonathan. "An Interview with Richard Ebright: The
    Who Investigation Members Were 'Participants in
    Disinformation' - Independent Science News: Food, Health and
    Agriculture Bioscience News." Independent Science News |
    Food, Health and Agriculture Bioscience News, May 24, 2021.
    https://www.independentsciencenews.org/commentaries/an-int

erview-with-richard-ebright-anthony-fauci-francis-collins-syste
matically-thwarted/

22. Jones, Will. "New Fauci Emails Reveal Lab Leak Cover-up Happening in Real Time." The Daily Sceptic, January 14, 2023. https://dailysceptic.org/2022/11/25/new-fauci-emails-re veal-lab-leak-cover-up-happening-in-real-time/

23. Andersen, Kristian G., Andrew Rambaut, W. Ian Lipkin, Ed- ward C. Holmes, and Robert F. Garry. "The Proximal Origin of SARS-COV-2." Nature News. Nature Publishing Group, March 17, 2020. https://www.nature.com/articles/s41591-020-0820-9

24. GT Staff Reporters. "Conspiracy Theory or Reasonable Skepti- cism? Why We Should Demand an Investigation into US Labs for Origins of COVID-19." Global Times, August 15, 2021. https: //www.globaltimes.cn/page/202108/1231519.shtml

25. Favorito, Maria. "Moderna Therapeutics Named to the WEF's Community of 'Global Growth Companies.'" Moderna Therapeutics Named to the WEF's Community of "Global Growth Companies", October 24, 2013. https://www.prnewswire.com/news-releases/moderna-therapeu tics-named-to-the-world-economic-forums-community-of-globa l-growth-companies-229077741.html

26. "Stéphane Bancel - Agenda Contributor." WEF. Accessed Feb- ruary 1, 2023. https://www.weforum.org/agenda/authors/steph ane-bancel

27. Zaleski, Andrew. "Bill and Melinda Gates Are Plac-

ing Bets on This Biotech in the Race to Develop a Zika Vaccine." CNBC. CNBC, May 19, 2017. https://www.cnbc.com/2017/05/18/bill-and-melinda-gates-bet-on-this-biotech-to-develop-zika-vaccine.html

28. Nathan-Kazis, Josh. "Moderna Gets US Government Grant to Develop Covid-19 Vaccine." Nasdaq, April 17, 2020. https://www.nasdaq.com/articles/moderna-gets-u.s.-government-grant-to-develop-covid-19-vaccine-2020-04-17

29. Forbes, Kristina. "Barda, Department of Defense, and SAB Biotherapeutics to Partner to Develop a Novel COVID-19 Therapeutic." Georgia Bio, April 6, 2020. https://gabio.org/barda-department-of-defense-and-sab-biotherapeutics-to-partner-to-develop-a-novel-covid-19-therapeutic/

30. "Trump Administration Announces Framework and Leadership for 'Operation Warp Speed'." US Department of Defense, May 15, 2020. https://www.defense.gov/News/Releases/Release/Article/2310750/trump-administration-announces-framework-and-leadership-for-operation-warp-speed/

31. Git, Awkward. Theleme Partners, Moderna and Rishi Sunak. Awkward Git's Newsletter, October 3, 2022. https://awkwardgit.substack.com/p/theleme-partners-moderna-and-rishi

32. Garside, Juliette. "Rishi Sunak Refuses to Say If He Will Profit from Moderna Covid Vaccine." The Guardian. Guardian News and Media, November 17, 2020.

https://www.theguardian.com/politics/2020/nov/17/rishi-sunak-refuses-to-say-if-he-will-profit-from-moderna-covid-vaccine

Chapter 6: Pandemic or Scamdemic? Part 2

1. "Covid in Sydney: Military Deployed to Help Enforce Lockdown." BBC News. BBC, July 30, 2021. https://www.bbc.com/news/world-australia-58021718

2. "Saskatchewan Issues New Provincial Emergency Order to Address Labour Mobility in the Healthcare System." September 13, 2021. https://www.saskatchewan.ca/government/news-and-media/2021/september/13/saskatchewan-issues-new-provincial-emergency-order-to-address-labour-mobility-in-the-healthcare-syst

3. Cadwell, Cate, Yawen Chen. "'Painful lesson': how a military-style lockdown unfolded in Wuhan." April 8, 2020. https://www.reuters.com/article/us-health-coronavirus-wuhan-scientists-i/painful-lesson-how-a-military-style-lockdown-unfolded-in-wuhan-idUSKBN21Q0KD

4. Brownstone Institute, Joakim Book, and Robert Blumen. "Fauci's 7-Hour Deposition: What We Know So far - Brownstone Institute." Brownstone Institute, December 1, 2022. https://brownstone.org/articles/faucis-7-hour-deposition-what-we-know-so-far/

5. Brennan, Jason, Chris Surprenant, and Eric Winsberg. "How Government Leaders Violated Their Epistemic Duties during the

SARS-COV-2 Crisis." SSRN, May 20, 2020. https://papers.ssr
n.com/sol3/papers.cfm?abstract_id=3605981

6. Blaylock, Russell. "COVID UPDATE: What is the truth?" National Library of Medicine, April 22, 2022. https://www.ncbi.n
lm.nih.gov/pmc/articles/PMC9062939/

7. Khamsi, Roxanne. 2022. "Did a Famous Doctor's COVID Shot Make His Cancer Worse?" The Atlantic. September 24. https://www.theatlantic.com/science/archive/2022/09/mr
na-covid-vaccine-booster-lymphoma-cancer/671308/

8. Ecarma, Caleb. 2021. "Joe Rogan and CNN Are Butting Heads Over 'Horse Dewormer' COVID Cure." Vanity Fair. October 22. https://www.vanityfair.com/news/2021/10/joe-rogan-c
nn-horse-dewormer-covid

9. Biden, Joe. 2021. "PolitiFact - Biden Says That Vaccinated People Can't Spread COVID-19. That's Not What CDC Says." @politifact. December 22. https://www.politifact.com/factchecks/2021/dec/22/joe-bi
den/biden-says-vaccinated-people-cant-spread-covid-19-/

10. O'Neill, Jesse. "Biden Admin Pushed to Bar Twitter Users for Covid 'Disinformation,' Files Show." *New York Post*, December 26, 2022. https://nypost.com/2022/12/26/biden-admin-pushe
d-to-ban-twitter-users-for-covid-disinformation/

11. Knight, Rochelle, Venexia Walker, Samantha Ip, Jennifer A. Cooper, Thomas Bolton, Spencer Keene, Rachel Denholm, et al. "Association of Covid-19 with Major Arterial and Venous

Thrombotic Diseases: A Population-Wide Cohort Study of 48 Million Adults in England and Wales." Circulation 146, no. 12 (2022): 892–906. https://doi.org/10.1161/circulationaha.122.0 60785

12. "Why Spike Protein Causes Abnormal, Foot-Long Blood Clots, 200 Symptoms – [Your]NEWS." 2023. [Your]NEWS. January 28. https://yournews.com/2022/11/06/2446774/why-spike-pr otein-causes-abnormal-foot-long-blood-clots-200-symptoms/

13. Altman NL, Berning AA, Saxon CE, Adamek KE, Wagner JA, Slavov D, Quaife RA, Gill EA, Minobe WA, Jonas ER, Carroll IA, Huebler SP, Raines J, Messenger JC, Ambardekar AV, Mestroni L, Rosenberg RM, Rove J, Campbell TB, Bristow MR. Myocardial Injury and Altered Gene Expression Associated With SARS-CoV-2 Infection or mRNA Vaccination. JACC Basic Transl Sci. 2022 Oct 19. doi: 10.1016/j.jacbts.2022.08.005. Epub ahead of print. PMID: 36281440; PMCID: PMC9581498. Myocardial Injury and Altered Gene Expression Associated With SARS-CoV-2 Infection or mRNA Vaccination - PMC (nih.gov)

14. Chudov, Igor. "Long Covid More Likely to Happen Soon after Vaccination." Long Covid MORE Likely to Happen SOON AFTER VACCINATION. Igor's Newsletter, November 19, 2 0 2 2 . https://igorchudov.substack.com/p/long-covid-more-likely-to-h appen?utm_source=post-email-title&publication_id=441185& post_id=85566857&isFreemail=true&utm_medium=email

15. Kimball, Spence. "Children's Hospitals Call on Biden

to Declare Emergency in Response to 'Unprece-dented' RSV Surge." CNBC. CNBC, November 18, 2022. https://www.cnbc.com/2022/11/18/biden-asked-to-decl are-emergency-over-rsv-flu-kids-hospitalizations.html

16. Chudov, Igor. "Is RSV More Severe in Covid Vaccinated Kids Due to Destroyed Hematopoietic Stem Cells?" Igor's Newsletter, November 18, 2022. https://igorchudov.substack.com/p/is-rsv-more-severe-in-covid -vaccinated?utm_source=post-email-title&publication_id=4411 85&post_id=85383334&isFreemail=true&utm_medium=emai l

17. Estep, Benjamin K., Charles J. Kuhlmann, Satoru Osuka, Gajen-dra W. Suryavanshi, Yoshiko Nagaoka-Kamata, Ciearria N. Samuel, Madison T. Blucas, Chloe E. Jepson, Paul A. Goepfert, and Masakazu Kamata. "Skewed Fate and Hematopoiesis of CD34+ Hspcs in Umbilical Cord Blood amid the COVID-19 Pandemic." iScience. Elsevier, November 10, 2022. https://ww w.cell.com/iscience/fulltext/S2589-0042(22)01816-8

18. Gayle, Damien. "Unvaccinated NHS Doctor Chal-lenges Sajid Javid over Compulsory Covid Jabs." The Guardian. Guardian News and Media, January 8, 2022. https://www.theguardian.com/politics/2022/jan/08/nhs -doctor-challenges-sajid-javid-over-covid-vaccination-rules

19. Chudov, Igor. "Australia's Former AMA President Defects, Exposes Covid Vaccines." Igor's Newsletter, December 20, 2022. https://igorchudov.substack.com/p/australias-former-am

a-president-defects

20. Shivaram, Deepa. "In the Fight against COVID, Health Workers Aren't Immune to Vaccine Misinformation." NPR. NPR, September 18, 2021. https://www.npr.org/2021/09/18/1037975289/unvaccinated-covid-19-vaccine-refuse-nurses-heath-care-workers

21. Zandrozni, Brandy, and Ben Collins. "As Vaccine Mandates Spread, Protests Follow - Some Spurred by Nurses." NBCNews.com. NBCUniversal News Group, 2021. https://www.nbcnews.com/tech/social-media/vaccine-mandates-spread-protests-follow-spurred-nurses-rcna1654

22. Taşkaldıran, Islay, et al. "Menstrual Changes after COVID-19 Infection and Covid-19 Vaccination." International journal of clinical practice. US National Library of Medicine. Accessed January 30, 2023. https://pubmed.ncbi.nlm.nih.gov/36349056/

23. Pfeiffer, Mary Beth. "The Missing Babies of Europe." The Missing Babies of Europe - by Mary Beth Pfeiffer. RESCUE with Michael Capuzzo, November 28, 2022. https://rescue.substack.com/p/the-missing-babies-of-europe

24. Shenai, Mahesh, et al. "Equivalency of Protection from Natural Immunity in Covid-19 Recovered versus Fully Vaccinated Persons: A Systematic Review and Pooled Analysis." Cureus. US National Library of Medicine. Accessed January 30, 2023. https://pubmed.ncbi.nlm.nih.gov/34868754/

25. Miltimore, Jon. "CDC: Natural Immunity Offered Stronger

Protection against Covid than Vaccines during Delta Wave: Jon Miltimore." FEE Freeman Article. Foundation for Economic Education, January 20, 2022. https://fee.org/articles/cdc-natural-immunity-offered-stronger-protection-against-covid-than-vaccines-during-delta-wave/

26. Malone MD, Robert. "MRNA Vaccines: The CIA and National Defense." Who is Robert Malone, October 27, 2022. https://rwmalonemd.substack.com/p/mrna-vaccines-the-cia-and-national?utm_source=post-email-title&publication_id=583200&post_id=80797095&isFreemail=true&utm_medium=email

27. McCullough, Peter. "US FDA Willfully Blind on the Safety of Covid-19 Vaccination." Courageous Discourse™ with Dr. Peter McCullough & John Leake. Courageous Discourse™ with Dr. Peter McCullough & John Leake, November 18, 2022. https://petermcculloughmd.substack.com/p/us-fda-willfully-blind-on-the-safety?utm_source=post-email-title&publication_id=1119676&post_id=85177035&isFreemail=true&utm_medium=email

28. Demasi, Maryanne. "FDA Oversight of Clinical Trials Is 'Grossly Inadequate," Say Experts." The BMJ. British Medical Journal Publishing Group, November 16, 2022. https://www.bmj.com/content/379/bmj.o2628

29. DePeau-Wilson, Michael. "Regulators Move against Two 'Misinformation' Doctors." Medical News. MedpageToday, November 1, 2022. https://www.medpagetoday.com/special-reports/exclusives/101529

30. Chossudovsky, Michel. "Bombshell Document Dump on Pfizer Vaccine Data." Global Research, December 7, 2022. https://www.globalresearch.ca/bombshell-document-dump-pfizer-vaccine-data/5763397

31. Git, Awkward. "UKHSA States That They Have No Proof SARS-COV-2 Causes Illness in Humans." UKHSA states that they have no proof SARS-CoV-2 causes illness in humans. Awkward Git's Newsletter, October 21, 2022. https://awkwardgit.substack.com/p/ukhsa-states-that-they-have-no-proof

32. Chudov, Igor. "Association Between Vaccines and EXCESS MORTALITY Getting Stronger -- and is Discussed in UK Parliament." Igor's Newsletter, November 6, 2022. https://igorchudov.substack.com/p/association-between-vaccines-and?utm_source=post-email-title&publication_id=441185&post_id=82945844&isFreemail=true&utm_medium=email

33. Sharff, Katie A, David M Dancoes, Jodi L Longueil, Eric S Johnson, and Paul F Lewis. "Risk of Myopericarditis following COVID-19 mRNA vaccination in a Large Integrated Health System: A Comparison of Completeness and Timeliness of Two Methods." medRxiv. Cold Spring Harbor Laboratory Press, January 1, 2021. https://www.medrxiv.org/content/10.1101/2021.12.21.21268209v1

34. Malone, Robert. "Tragic: 14-Year Old Vaccine Myocarditis Victim." Tragic: 14-Year Old Vaccine Myocarditis Victim. Who is Robert Malone, November 23, 2022. https://rwmalonemd.substack.com/p/tragic-14-year-old-vaccine

-myocarditis?utm_source=post-email-title&publication_id=583
200&post_id=86402682&isFreemail=true&utm_medium=ema
il

35. McCullough, Peter. "SARS-COV-2 Spike Protein Found in the Human Nucleus." Courageous Discourse™ with Dr. Peter McCullough & John Leake. Courageous Discourse™, November 14, 2022. https://petermcculloughmd.substack.com/p/sars-cov-2-spike-pr otein-found-in?utm_source=post-email-title&publication_id=1 119676&post_id=84481153&isFreemail=true&utm_medium= email

36. Dalgleish, Angus. "As an Oncologist I Am Seeing People with Stable Cancer Rapidly Progress after Being Forced to Have a Booster." The Daily Sceptic, November 27, 2022. https://dailysceptic.org/2022/11/26/as-an-oncologist-i-am-seein g-people-with-stable-cancer-rapidly-progress-after-being-forced-t o-have-a-booster/

37. Khamsi, Roxanne. "Did a Famous Doctor's Covid Shot Make His Cancer Worse?" The Atlantic. Atlantic Media Company, October 6, 2022. https://www.theatlantic.com/science/archive/2022 /09/mrna-covid-vaccine-booster-lymphoma-cancer/671308/

38. Mercola, Joseph. "Is Ivermectin a Cancer Solution?" www.theepochtimes.com, December 21, 2022. https://www.theepochtimes.com/health/is-ivermectin-a-cancer -solution_4463739.html?utm_source=brightnoe&src_src=brig htnoe&utm_campaign=bright-2022-12-20&src_cmp=bright-2

022-12-20&utm_medium=email&est=RBta7xlbEiNkzQy6civz
pvJwib9jmOX51rfRdToeTGVw8TSFx5WEJOmSQzhNtPwY
%2BW%2Bp3Q

39. Fournier, Dan. "Canadian Doctors Still under Attack for
Exposing Stillbirths Caused by C19 Vaccines." Dan Fournier's
Inconvenient   Truths,   November   27,   2022.
https://fournier.substack.com/p/bc-doctors-still-under-attack-f
or?utm_source=post-email-title&publication_id=1075505&po
st_id=87166368&isFreemail=true&utm_medium=email

40. Madrid, Pablo Campra. "GRAPHENE OXIDE DETECTION
IN AQUEOUS SUSPENSION OBSERVATIONAL STUDY
IN OPTICAL AND ELECTRON MICROSCOPY: Official
Interim Report in English (University of Almeria).PDF." Doc-
Droid, June 2021. https://www.docdroid.net/Ov1M99x/officia
l-interim-report-in-english-university-of-almeria-pdf

41. Git, Awkward. "MHRA admitted in FOI protecting Pfizer's
reputation is more important than the public knowing about
their mRNA vaccines." Awkward Git's Newsletter, October
27, 2022. https://awkwardgit.substack.com/p/mhra-admitted-i
n-foi-protecting-pfizers

42. Chudov, Igor. "Demand for Unvaccinated Blood Is Real,
Doctors Acknowledge Grumpily." Demand for Unvaccinated
Blood is Real, Doctors Acknowledge Grumpily. Igor's
Newsletter,   November   17,   2022.
https://igorchudov.substack.com/p/demand-for-unvaccinated-b
lood-is?utm_source=post-email-title&publication_id=441185&

post_id=85190155&isFreemail=true&utm_medium=email

43. Malone, Robert W. "MRNA Vaccines: The CIA and National Defense." mRNA Vaccines: The CIA and National Defense. Who is Robert Malone, October 27, 2022. https://rwmalonemd.substack.com/p/mrna-vaccines-the-cia-and-national?utm_source=post-email-title&publication_id=583200&post_id=80797095&isFreemail=true&utm_medium=email

44. Malone, Robert W. "MRNA Vaccines: The CIA and National Defense." mRNA Vaccines: The CIA and National Defense. Who is Robert Malone, October 27, 2022. https://rwmalonemd.substack.com/p/mrna-vaccines-the-cia-and-national?utm_source=post-email-title&publication_id=583200&post_id=80797095&isFreemail=true&utm_medium=email

45. McKay, Scott. "Birx's Book Damages Trump and Disqualifies Pence". The American Spectator, July 21, 2022. https://spectator.org/birxs-book-damages-trump-and-disqualifies-pence/

46. Waters, Jesse. "Fauci and Birx Make Startling Admissions about Vaccinations | Fox News Video." Fox News. FOX News Network. Accessed January 31, 2023. https://www.foxnews.com/video/6310008251112

47. Islam, Faisal. "How Much Economic Damage Would a Circuit-Breaker Lockdown Do?" BBC News. BBC, October 14, 2020. https://www.bbc.co.uk/news/business-54543654

48. Volokh, Eugene, Eric Boehm, Elizabeth Nolan Brown, Phillip W. Magness, Charles Oliver, and Jacob Sullum. "No-Lockdown Sweden Seemingly Tied for Lowest All-Causes Mortality in OECD since Covid Arrived." Reason.com, January 10, 2023. https://reason.com/volokh/2023/01/10/no-lockdown-sweden-seemingly-tied-for-lowest-all-causes-mortality-in-oecd-since-covid-arrived/

49. Gopinath, Gita. "The Great Lockdown: Worst Economic Downturn since the Great Depression." IMF. Accessed January 31, 2023. https://www.imf.org/en/Blogs/Articles/2020/04/14/blog-weo-the-great-lockdown-worst-economic-downturn-since-the-great-depression

50. Clevely, Marigold, and Brian Steere. "Evidence of Collateral Damage from Lockdowns Consolidates." Alliance for Natural Health International, November 13, 2020. https://www.anhinternational.org/news/evidence-of-collateral-damage-from-lockdowns-consolidates/

51. "An International Treaty on Pandemic Prevention and Preparedness." Consilium, January 12, 2023. https://www.consilium.europa.eu/en/policies/coronavirus/pandemic-treaty/

52. Aginam, Obijiofor. "The World Health Assembly Special Session and the Pandemic Treaty Controversy." Our World. Accessed January 31, 2023. https://ourworld.unu.edu/en/the-world-health-assembly-special-session-and-the-pandemic-treaty-controversy

53. Leake, John. "Who Is Dr. Asish Jha (President Biden's Covid Czar)?" Courageous Discourse™ with Dr. Peter McCullough & John Leake, November 25, 2022. https://petermcculloughmd.substack.com/p/who-is-dr-asish-jha -president-bidens?utm_source=substack&utm_medium=email

54. Malone, Robert. "Mass Formation Psychosis." MASS FORMA-TION PSYCHOSIS - by Robert W Malone MD, MS. Who is Robert Malone, December 9, 2021. https://rwmalonemd.subs tack.com/p/mass-formation-psychosis

55. Deagel.com. "List of Countries Forecast 2025." October 26, 2014. http://web.archive.org/web/20170730094149/http://w ww.deagel.com:80/country/forecast.aspx

56. Weintz, Lori, Thomas Harrington, and Gabrielle Bauer. "The Great Overreaction - Brownstone Institute." Brownstone Insti-tute, December 18, 2022. https://brownstone.org/articles/the-g reat-overreaction/

Chapter 7: It's the sUN Driving the Climate, Not hUmaNs

1. "Climate Change Widespread, Rapid, and Intensifying." IPCC, August 9, 2021. https://www.ipcc.ch/2021/08/09/ar6-wg1-20 210809-pr/

2. "What Is Climate Change?" United Nations. United Nations. Accessed February 1, 2023. https://www.un.org/en/climatecha nge/what-is-climate-change

3. McConnell, Tristan. "The Maldives Is Being Swallowed by the Sea. Can It Adapt?" Environment. National Geographic, January 20, 2022. https://www.nationalgeographic.com/environment/article/the-maldives-is-being-swallowed-by-the-sea-can-it-adapt

4. Morrison, Chris. "41% Of Climate Scientists Don't Believe in Catastrophic Climate Change, Major New Poll Finds." The Daily Sceptic, November 12, 2022. https://dailysceptic.org/2022/11/11/41-of-climate-scientists-dont-believe-in-catastrophic-climate-change-major-new-poll-finds/

5. ITV News. "Lincolnshire Registers Hottest Ever UK Temperature." ITV News, July 19, 2022. https://www.itv.com/news/calendar/2022-07-19/lincolnshire-registers-joint-hottest-ever-uk-temperature

6. Morrison, Chris. "South Pole Hits Record Cold November Temperatures." The Daily Sceptic, November 20, 2022. https://dailysceptic.org/2022/11/20/south-pole-hits-record-cold-november-temperatures/

7. Morrison, Chris. "Fresh Doubts Emerge about 40.3°C UK Temperature Record next to Airfield Runway." The Daily Sceptic, November 28, 2022. https://dailysceptic.org/2022/11/27/fresh-doubts-emerge-about-40-3c-u-k-temperature-record-next-to-airfield-runway/

8. Black, Richard. "Global Warming 'Confirmed' by Independent Study." BBC News. BBC, October 21, 2011. https://www.bbc.

com/news/science-environment-15373071

9. "The Heat Is On." The Economist. The Economist Newspaper. Accessed February 1, 2023. https://www.economist.com/scienc e-and-technology/2011/10/22/the-heat-is-on

10. "Cooling the Warming Debate: Major New Analysis Confirms ... - Sciencedaily." Science Daily, October 21, 2011. https://www.s ciencedaily.com/releases/2011/10/111021144716.htm

11. Rose, David. "Scientists Who Said Climate Change Sceptics Had Been Proved Wrong Accused of Hiding Truth by Colleague." Daily Mail Online. Associated Newspapers, October 30, 2011. https://www.dailymail.co.uk/sciencetech/article-2055191/Scien tists-said-climate-change-sceptics-proved-wrong-accused-hiding -truth-colleague.html

12. Pearce, Fred. "Leaked Climate Change Emails Scientist 'Hid' Data Flaws." The Guardian. Guardian News and Media, February 1, 2010. https://www.theguardian.com/environment/2010 /feb/01/leaked-emails-climate-jones-chinese

13. Taylor, James. "Climategate 2.0: New E-Mails Rock The Global Warming Debate." Forbes. Forbes Magazine, August 25, 2019. https://www.forbes.com/sites/jamestaylor/2011/11/23/climate gate-2-0-new-e-mails-rock-the-global-warming-debate/?sh=1759 068b27ba

14. Morrison, Chris. "Climate Models Can Never Work, Says Computer Modeller." The Daily Sceptic, November 14, 2022. https://dailysceptic.org/2022/11/14/climate-models-can

-never-work-says-computer-modeller/

15. Harrington, Samantha. "Scientists agree: Climate change is real and caused by people." Yale Climate Connections, October 17, 2022. https://yaleclimateconnections.org/2022/02/scientists-agree-climate-change-is-real-and-caused-by-people/

16. Lee, Howard. "How Earth's Climate Changes Naturally (and Why Things Are Different Now)." Quanta Magazine, April 15, 2021. https://www.quantamagazine.org/how-earths-climate-changes-naturally-and-why-things-are-different-now-20200721/

17. "A More Active Sun: Solar Cycle 25 off to a Fast Start!" Almanac.com, March 8, 2022. https://www.almanac.com/solar-cycle-25-sun-heating

18. "What Are Solar Cycles, and How Do They Affect Weather?" Almanac.com, January 10, 2023. https://www.almanac.com/what-are-solar-cycles-and-how-do-they-affect-weather

19. Hartley, Eve. "What Are the Major Contributors to Climate Change?" Yahoo! News. Yahoo!, October 22, 2021. https://news.yahoo.com/what-are-the-major-contributors-to-climate-change-204535627.html

20. Shellenberger, Michael. "Unreliable Nature of Solar and Wind Makes Electricity More Expensive, New Study Finds." Forbes. Forbes Magazine, April 24, 2019. https://www.forbes.com/sites/michaelshellenberger/2019/04/22/unreliable-nature-of-solar-and-wind-makes-electricity-much-more-expensive-major-new-study-finds/?sh=497192524f59

21. Merriman, Joel. "Are Wind Turbines a Significant Threat to Birds?" American Bird Conservancy, March 2, 2021. https://abcbirds.org/blog21/wind-turbines-are-threat-to-birds/

22. Cross, Lucienne. "See the forest for more than the trees – why reforestation isn't working." Inhabitat, August 6, 2019. https://inhabitat.com/see-the-forest-for-more-than-the-trees-why-reforestation-isnt-working/

23. Howard, Brian Clark. "Freakonomics Authors Make Controversial Case for Geoengineering." Environment. National Geographic, May 3, 2021. https://www.nationalgeographic.com/environment/article/freakonomics-authors-make-controversial-case-for-geoengineering

24. Irfan, Umair. "Will Carbon Capture and Storage Ever Work?" Scientific American. Scientific American, May 25, 2017. https://www.scientificamerican.com/article/will-carbon-capture-and-storage-ever-work/

25. French, David. "Apocalypse Delayed." National Review. National Review, January 28, 2016. https://www.nationalreview.com/2016/01/al-gore-doomsday-clock-expires-climate-change-fanatics-wrong-again/

26. Perry, Mark J. "18 Spectacularly Wrong Predictions Made around the Time of the First Earth Day in 1970, Expect More This Year." AEI, April 21, 2015. https://www.aei.org/carpe-diem/18-spectacularly-wrong-predictions-made-around-the-time-of-the-first-earth-day-in-1970-expe

ct-more-this-year/

27. Morrison, Chris. "UKHSA Chief Jenny Harries Attempts to Blame Excess Deaths on Climate Change." The Daily Sceptic, November 16, 2022. https://dailysceptic.org/2022/11/16/ukhsa-chief-jenny-harries-attempts-to-blame-excess-deaths-on-climate-change/

28. Shine, Ian. "7 Unexpected Side-Effects of Climate Change." WEF, December 22, 2022. https://www.weforum.org/agenda/2022/12/strange-unexpected-effects-climate-change/

29. Giuliani, Matteo, Jonathan R. Lamontagne, Mohamad I. Hejazi, Patrick M. Reed, and Andrea Castelletti. "Unintended Consequences of Climate Change Mitigation for African River Basins." Nature News. Nature Publishing Group, January 31, 2022. https://www.nature.com/articles/s41558-021-01262-9

30. Lopez, Mariana. "Making the Connection between Mobile Money and Climate Change." Mobile for Development, December 18, 2019. https://www.gsma.com/mobilefordevelopment/blog/making-the-connection-between-mobile-money-and-climate-change/

31. Morrison, Chris. "Net Zero Is Marxism Dressed up as Environmentalism." The Daily Sceptic, January 17, 2023. https://dailysceptic.org/2023/01/17/net-zero-is-marxism-dressed-up-as-environmentalism/

32. Weisenthal, Joe. "The 10 Most-Respected Global Warming Skeptics." Business Insider. Accessed February 1, 2023.

https://www.businessinsider.com/the-ten-most-important-clim
ate-change-skeptics-2009-7?r=US&IR=T%23ivar-giaever-5

33. Durden, Tyler. "'Zombie' Virus Reanimated after 50,000 Years in Siberian Permafrost." ZeroHedge. Accessed February 1, 2023. https://www.zerohedge.com/medical/zombie-virus-reani mated-after-50000-years-siberian-permafrost

34. Fears, Darryl. "Dawn of Super Crab." The Washington Post. WP Company, April 7, 2013. https://www.washingtonpost.com/national/health-science/201 3/04/07/a0c29f48-972f-11e2-b68f-dc5c4b47e519_story.html?_ =ddid-3-1674161340

35. Tarantola, Andrew. "Antarctica Is Losing So Much Ice It's Throwing Off Earth's Gravity." Gizmodo. Gizmodo, September 30, 2014. https://gizmodo.com/antarctica-is-losing-so-much-ic e-its-throwing-off-earth-1640915248

Chapter 8: You WILL Eat the Bugs

1. "8 Predictions for the World in 2030." WEF, November 12, 2016. http://wef.ch/2gmBN7M https://www.facebook.com/watch/ ?v=10153920524981479&ref=sharing]

2. Hubert, Antoine. "Why We Need to Give Insects the Role They Deserve in Our Food Systems." WEF, July 12, 2021. https://www.weforum.org/agenda/2021/07/why-we-nee d-to-give-insects-the-role-they-deserve-in-our-food-systems/

3. Fleming, Sean. "Good Grub: Why We Might Be Eating Insects

Soon." WEF, July 16, 2018. https://www.weforum.org/agenda/2018/07/good-grub-why-we-might-be-eating-insects-soon/

4. "Sustainable Consumption: Stakeholder Perspectives." WEF, November 22, 2013. https://www.weforum.org/reports/sustainable-consumption-stakeholder-perspectives

5. Durst, P., Johnson, D., Leslie, R., Shono, K., *Edible Forest Insects: Humans Bite Back*. Food and Agriculture Organization of the United Nations: Bangkok, 2010. https://www.fao.org/3/i1380e/i1380e00.htm

6. Ritchie, Hannah. "Half of the World's Habitable Land Is Used for Agriculture." Our World in Data, November 11, 2019. https://ourworldindata.org/global-land-for-agriculture

7. Baker, Aryn. "How Humans Eating Insects Could Help Save the Planet." Time. Time, February 26, 2021. https://time.com/5942290/eat-insects-save-planet/

8. Beans, Carolyn. "Salted Ants. Ground Crickets. Why You Should Try Edible Insects." The Washington Post. WP Company, November 29, 2022. https://www.washingtonpost.com/health/2022/11/27/eating-insects-good-for-you/

9. Godwin, Richard. "If We Want to Save the Planet, the Future of Food Is Insects." The Guardian. Guardian News and Media, May 8, 2021. https://www.theguardian.com/food/2021/may/08/if-we-want-to-save-the-planet-the-future-of-food-is-insects

10. Huis, Arnold van. "Edible insects are the future? Proceedings of

the Nutrition Society." Cambridge Core. Cambridge University Press, February 24, 2016. https://www.cambridge.org/core/journals/proceedings-of-the-nutrition-society/article/edible-insects-are-the-future/206E43F1C95FCA2E67EF04950321414E

11. Beals, Rachel Koning. "Davos May Devote Time to Climate Change but Polluting Jets and Limos Common." MarketWatch, May 24, 2022. https://www.marketwatch.com/story/at-davos-are-leaders-private-jets-and-limos-actually-hurting-climate-change-efforts-11653414210

12. "Radiohead's Pioneering Research + 2008 Carbon Neutral Tour." Ecolibrium, February 22, 2021. https://ecolibrium.earth/case-study/radiohead-2008-carbon-neutral-tour/

13. Fisher, Paul. "Step inside the Eco-Friendly Home of Ed Begley Jr. and Rachelle Carson-Begley." Ventura Blvd, April 17, 2022. https://venturablvd.goldenstate.is/step-inside-the-eco-friendly-home-of-ed-begley-jr-and-rachelle-carson-begley/

14. Scobie, Omid. "Prince Charles Praises William and Harry for Their Environmental Activism." Harper's BAZAAR. Harper's BAZAAR, January 4, 2022. https://www.harpersbazaar.com/celebrity/latest/a38665635/prince-charles-praises-harry-william-environmentalism/

15. Betz, Bradford. "Prince Harry, Leonardo DiCaprio and Other Celebrities Who Are Hypocritical on Climate

Change." Fox News. FOX News Network, January 30, 2020. https://www.foxnews.com/entertainment/celebrities-hypocritical-climate-change

16. Beals, Rachel Koning. "Davos May Devote Time to Climate Change but Polluting Jets and Limos Common." MarketWatch, May 24, 2022. https://www.marketwatch.com/story/at-davos-are-leaders-private-jets-and-limos-actually-hurting-climate-change-efforts-11653414210

17. Komi, Daniel Elieh Ali, et al. "Chitin and Its Effects on Inflammatory and Immune Responses." Clinical reviews in allergy & immunology. US National Library of Medicine, April 2018. https://pubmed.ncbi.nlm.nih.gov/28251581/]

18. Gray, Mia, and Anna Barford. "The Depths of the Cuts: The Uneven Geography of Local Government Austerity." Cambridge Journal of Regions, Economy and Society 11, no. 3 (2018): 541–63. https://doi.org/10.1093/cjres/rsy019

19. Gray, Mia, and Anna Barford. "The Depths of the Cuts: The Uneven Geography of Local Government Austerity." Cambridge Journal of Regions, Economy and Society 11, no. 3 (2018): 541–63. https://doi.org/10.1093/cjres/rsy019

20. Way, L. Randall. "MMT Blog #42: Introduction to the Job Guarantee or Employer of Last Resort." New Economic Perspectives, March 19, 2012. https://neweconomicperspectives.org/2012/03/mmp-blog-42-i

ntroduction-the-the-job-guarantee-or-employer-of-last-resort.ht
ml

21. Parlier, Spencer. "Martin Luther King Jr. on Universal Basic Income." Heavy.com. Heavy, October 25, 2022. https://heavy.co
m/news/2019/06/mlk-jr-universal-basic-income/

22. Naidu, Nikayla. "Why We Need Modern Monetary Theory
(MMT) and Why It Needs Universal Basic Income (UBI)." SPII,
September 15, 2021. https://spii.org.za/information-pertaining
-to-the-basic-income-grant-ubi/

23. Fazekas, Lee. "The Problem with Universal Basic Income." Communist Party USA, May 4, 2020. https://cpusa.org/article/the-p
roblem-with-universal-basic-income/

24. "About Bis - Overview." The Bank for International Settlements,
January 1, 2005. https://www.bis.org/about/index.htm

25. Wood, Patrick. "The Dark Past of the Bank for International Settlements." Truth Comes to Light, February 23,
2021. https://truthcomestolight.com/the-dark-past-of-the-ban
k-for-international-settlements/

26. Wan, Samuel. "The BIS Wants 'Absolute Control' of Your Money
via Central Bank Digital Currencies." Bitcoinist.com, July 10,
2021. https://bitcoinist.com/the-bis-wants-absolute-control-of
-your-money-via-central-bank-digital-currencies/

27. Georgieva, Kristalina. "The Future of Money: Gearing up for
Central Bank Digital Currency." IMF, February 9, 2022.

https://www.imf.org/en/News/Articles/2022/02/09/sp020922
-the-future-of-money-gearing-up-for-central-bank-digital-curren
cy

28. "Fact Sheet: White House Releases First-Ever Comprehensive
    Framework for Responsible Development of Digital Assets." The
    White House. The United States Government, September 16,
    2   0   2   2   .
    https://www.whitehouse.gov/briefing-room/statements-releases
    /2022/09/16/fact-sheet-white-house-releases-first-ever-compreh
    ensive-framework-for-responsible-development-of-digital-assets
    /

29. "UK Central Bank Digital Currency." Bank of England, August
    12, 2022. https://www.bankofengland.co.uk/digital-currencies

30. Malone, Robert. "Global News: A Global Passport for Vaccines
    and Carbon Tracking." Global News: A Global Passport for
    Vaccines and Carbon Tracking. Who is Robert Malone,
    November   22,   2022.
    https://rwmalonemd.substack.com/p/global-news-a-global-pass
    port-for?utm_source=post-email-title&publication_id=583200
    &post_id=86168329&isFreemail=true&utm_medium=email

31. U.S. Mission Japan. "Covid-19 Vaccine Requirements for Travel
    to the United States." US Embassy & Consulates in Japan, No-
    vember 30, 2022. https://jp.usembassy.gov/us-travel-requireme
    nts/

32. Chudov, Igor. "Should Individualism Be Medicated Away to Be

Replaced by 'Welfarism?" Igor's Newsletter, November 22, 2022. https://igorchudov.substack.com/p/should-individualism-be-m edicated?utm_source=post-email-title&publication_id=441185 &post_id=86021257&isFreemail=true&utm_medium=email

33. Henderson, Emily. "Researchers aim to develop edible plant-based mRNA vaccines." News, September 16, 2021. https://www.news-medical.net/news/20210916/Researc hers-aim-to-develop-edible-plant-based-mRNA-vaccines.aspx

34. Chudov, Igor. "Vaccine-like 'Inoculation' of Minds with 'Weakened Forms of Misinformation.'" Vaccine-like "Inoculation" of Minds with "Weakened Forms of Misinformation". Igor's Newsletter, October 30, 2022. https://igorchudov.substack.com/p/vaccine-like-inoculation-of -minds?utm_source=post-email-title&publication_id=441185 &post_id=68983499&isFreemail=true&utm_medium=email

35. Malone, Robert. "Transcommunism Is Coming." Transcommunism is coming. - by Robert W Malone MD, MS. Who is Robert Malone, November 8, 2022. https://rwmalonemd.substack.com/p/transcommunism-is-comi ng?utm_source=post-email-title&publication_id=583200&post _id=82834768&isFreemail=true&utm_medium=email

36. Schepers, Frans. "Healing the Planet: Rewilding and the Covid-19 Pandemic." Rewilding Europe, February 4, 2021. https://rewildingeurope.com/blog/healing-the-planet-re wilding-and-the-covid-19-pandemic/

37.

"Government Takes Historic Step towards Net-Zero with End of Sale of New Petrol and Diesel Cars by 2030." GOV.UK, November 18, 2020. https://www.gov.uk/government/news/government-takes-histo ric-step-towards-net-zero-with-end-of-sale-of-new-petrol-and-di esel-cars-by-2030

38. HM Government. "Transitioning to Zero Emission Cars and Vans: 2035 Delivery Plan." assets.publishing.service.gov.uk, 2 0 2 1 . https://assets.publishing.service.gov.uk/government/uploads/sy stem/uploads/attachment_data/file/1005301/transitioning-to-z ero-emission-cars-vans-2035-delivery-plan.pdf

39. Hinchliffe, Tim. "'Embrace the Fourth Industrial Revolution', Winners Take All: Klaus Schwab, APEC." The Sociable, November 22, 2022. https://sociable.co/government-and-policy/embra ce-fourth-industrial-revolution-klaus-schwab-apec/

40. "Forum Members." WEF. Accessed January 31, 2023. https://w ww.weforum.org/communities/forum-members

41. "Agenda 21." United Nations, 1992. https://www.un.org/esa/d sd/agenda21/res_agenda21_00.shtml

42. Koire, Rosa. *Behind the Green Mask: UN Agenda 21*. Santa Rosa, CA: Post Sustainability Institute Press, 2011.

43. "Agenda 21: Sustainable Development Knowledge Platform." United Nations. Accessed January 31, 2023. https://sustainabl edevelopment.un.org/outcomedocuments/agenda21

44. "About Us." ICLEI. Accessed January 31, 2023. https://iclei.or g/about_iclei_2/

45. Urban Land Institute. "Uli Highlights Business Case for Real Estate Alignment with UN Sustainable Development Goals." ULI Americas, April 19, 2021. https://americas.uli.org/210419sdgre port/

46. Ewing, Reid H., and Geoffrey Anderson. *Growing Cooler: The Evidence on Urban Development and Climate Change*. Washington, D.C.: ULI, 2008. https://www.google.co.uk/books/edition/Growing_Cooler/5cs kAQAAMAAJ?hl=en&gbpv=0&bsq=Growing%20Cooler%20t he%20Evidence%20on%20Urban%20Development%20and%20 Climate%20Change.%20Washington,%20D.C.:%20ULI,%2020 08.

47. Gomez, Christian. *Exposing The 2030 Agenda*. The John Birch Society.   2022: https://www.google.com/url?sa=t&rct=j&q=&esrc=s&source= web&cd=&ved=2ahUKEwiF8d6G2vL8AhUzk4kEHZQjCrA QFnoECAoQAQ&url=https%3A%2F%2Fjbs.org%2Fassets%2F pdf%2FExposing-2030-Agenda-Booklet.pdf&usg=AOvVaw38 UzcWy5HfdfNvX4M3Ctd2

Chapter 9: Narrative Control

1. Little, Becky. "How the US Got so Many Confederate Monuments." History.com. A&E Television Networks, August 17, 2017. https://www.history.com/news/how-the-u-s-got-so-man

y-confederate-monuments

2. Davis, Phil. "George Washington Monument in Druid Hill Park Spray-Painted with 'Destroy Racists,' Anti-Police Sentiment." Baltimore Sun, June 21, 2020. https://www.baltimoresun.com/maryland/baltimore-city/bs-md-ci-baltimore-washington-monument-vandalized-20200621-h5tbqr6jazb7dfn645to5wb37a-story.html

3. Cramer, Maria. "Chicago Lists Lincoln Statues among Monuments to Review." *The New York Times*, February 18, 2021. https://www.nytimes.com/2021/02/18/us/chicago-statues-abraham-lincoln.html

4. Mak, Tim. "D.C. Statue of Lincoln Standing over a Formerly Enslaved Man Sparks Controversy." NPR, June 27, 2020. https://www.npr.org/2020/06/27/884213464/dc-statue-of-lincoln-standing-over-a-formerly-enslaved-man-sparks-controversy

5. Associated Press. "San Francisco School Board Drops Plan to Rename 'Injustice-Linked' Schools." The Guardian. Guardian News and Media, April 7, 2021. https://www.theguardian.com/us-news/2021/apr/07/san-francisco-school-board-schools-rename

6. Onibada, Ade. "Statues in the US and around the World Are Being Beheaded and Torn down amid Black Lives Matter Protests." BuzzFeed News, June 10, 2020. https://www.buzzfeednews.com/article/adeonibada/statues-torn-down-monuments-us-uk-columbus-churchill-colston

7. Andrew, Scottie, and Anna Sturla. "A Statue of Frederick Douglass Was Toppled over the Fourth of July Weekend, the Anniversary of His Famous Speech." CNN. Cable News Network, July 7, 2020. https://www.cnn.com/2020/07/06/us/frederick-douglass-statue-toppled-trnd/index.html

8. Brenan, Megan. "Americans' Trust in Media Dips to Second Lowest on Record." Gallup.com. Gallup, November 20, 2021. https://news.gallup.com/poll/355526/americans-trust-media-dips-second-lowest-record.aspx

9. "Trusted News Initiative - beyond Fake News." BBC News. BBC. Accessed January 31, 2023. https://www.bbc.co.uk/beyondfakenews/trusted-news-initiative/

10. Mercola, Joseph. "Who Is behind the Trusted News Initiative?" Organic Consumers Association, August 20, 2022. https://www.organicconsumers.org/news/who-behind-trusted-news-initiative

11. Ha, Anthony. "Google Unveils Its $300M News Initiative." TechCrunch, March 20, 2018. https://techcrunch.com/2018/03/20/google-news-initiative/

12. Leetaru, Kalev. "The Daily Mail Snopes Story and Fact Checking the Fact Checkers." Forbes. Forbes Magazine, December 30, 2016. https://www.forbes.com/sites/kalevleetaru/2016/12/22/the-daily-mail-snopes-story-and-fact-checking-the-fact-checkers/?sh=11dd929227f8

13. Jones, Dean Sterling. "The Cofounder of the Fact-Checking Site Snopes Was Writing Plagiarized Articles under a Fake Name." BuzzFeed News, August 27, 2021. https://www.buzzfeednews.com/article/deansterlingjones/snopes-cofounder-plagiarism-mikkelson

14. Leetaru, Kalev. "The Lessons of Poynter's Retracted 'Unreliable News' Blacklist." Real Clear Politics, May 18, 2019. https://www.realclearpolitics.com/articles/2019/05/18/the_lessons_of_poynters_retracted_unreliable_news_blacklist.html#

15. Ronnie. "Poynter: Self Claimed 'Factchecking Group' Funded by Media Giants." Canuck Law, October 2, 2021. https://canucklaw.ca/poynter-self-claimed-factchecking-group-funded-by-media-giants/

16. Schwab, Tim. "Journalism's Gates Keepers." Columbia Journalism Review, August 21, 2020. https://www.cjr.org/criticism/gates-foundation-journalism-funding.php

17. Tarfe, Akshay. "Why Are Indians so Angry at Bill Gates?" The Diplomat, June 30, 2021. https://thediplomat.com/2021/06/why-are-indians-so-angry-at-bill-gates/

18. Mookim, Mohit. "The World Loses under Bill Gates' Vaccine Colonialism." Wired. Conde Nast, May 19, 2021. https://www.wired.com/story/opinion-the-world-loses-under-bill-gates-vaccine-colonialism/

19. Reuters Staff. "FACT Check: RFID Microchips Will Not Be Injected with the COVID-19 Vaccine, Altered Video Features Bill

and Melinda Gates and Jack Ma." Reuters. Thomson Reuters, December 4, 2020. https://www.reuters.com/article/uk-factcheck-vaccine-microchip-gates-ma/fact-check-rfid-microchips-will-not-be-injected-with-the-covid-19-vaccine-altered-video-features-bill-and-melinda-gates-and-jack-ma-idUSKBN28E286

20. Harari, Yuval Noah. "Yuval Noah Harari: The World after Coronavirus: Free to Read." Financial Times, March 20, 2020. https://www.ft.com/content/19d90308-6858-11ea-a3c9-1fe6fedcca75

21. Hoban, Virgie. "'Discredit, Disrupt, and Destroy': FBI Records Acquired by the Library Reveal Violent Surveillance of Black Leaders, Civil Rights Organizations." UC Berkeley Library, January 18, 2021. https://www.lib.berkeley.edu/about/news/fbi

22. Redshaw, Megan. "Conflict of Interest: Reuters 'Fact Checks' Covid-Related Social Media Posts, but Fails to Disclose Ties to Pfizer, WEF." Children's Health Defense, August 11, 2021. https://childrenshealthdefense.org/defender/reuters-fact-check-covid-social-media-pfizer-world-economic-forum/

23. "James Smith." Pfizer. Accessed January 31, 2023. https://www.pfizer.com/people/leadership/board_of_directors/james_smith

24. IFCN code of Principles. Accessed January 31, 2023. https://ifcncodeofprinciples.poynter.org/application/public/reuters/DC531AD7-1DA8-5D81-5B7D-5A170F4F8FB7

25. Ceci, Stephen J. "The Psychology of Fact-Checking." Scientific American. Scientific American, October 25,

2020. https://www.scientificamerican.com/article/the-psychol
ogy-of-fact-checking1/

26. "77th Brigade | The British Army." Accessed February 1,
2023. https://www.army.mod.uk/who-we-are/formations-divis
ions-brigades/6th-united-kingdom-division/77-brigade/

27. Seitz, Amanda. "Disinformation Board to Tackle Russia,
Migrant Smugglers." AP NEWS. Associated Press, April 28,
2   0   2   2   .
https://apnews.com/article/russia-ukraine-immigration-media-e
urope-misinformation-4e873389889bb1d9e2ad8659d9975e9d

28. Editorial Board. "Opinion | the Disinformation Governance
Board, Disavowed." The Wall Street Journal. Dow Jones &
Company,   May   18,   2022.
https://www.wsj.com/articles/the-disinformation-governance-b
oard-disavowed-nina-jankowicz-homeland-security-mary-poppi
ns-11652910532

29. Kaplan,   Talia.   "FCC   Commissioner   Says   Biden's
'Disinformation Board' Is 'Unconstitutional'." Fox Business,
May   9,   2022.
https://www.foxbusiness.com/politics/fcc-commissioner-blasts
-bidens-disinformation-board-as-orwellian-and-un-american

30. Ross, Chuck. "DHS Solicited Twitter to 'Become Involved' in Disinfo Board." Washington Free Beacon, June 10,
2022. https://freebeacon.com/biden-administration/dhs-solicit
ed-twitter-to-become-involved-in-disinfo-board/

31. Reuters Staff. "Financial Market Website Zero Hedge Knocked off Twitter over Coronavirus Story." Reuters. Thomson Reuters, February 2, 2020. https://www.reuters.com/article/china-health-twitter/financial-market-website-zero-hedge-knocked-off-twitter-over-coronavirus-story-idINL4N2A20FU

32. Klippenstein, Ken, and Lee Fang. "Leaked Documents Outline DHS's Plans to Police Disinformation." The Intercept, October 31, 2022. https://theintercept.com/2022/10/31/social-media-disinformation-dhs/

33. PDNordic. "CIA's Operation Mockingbird a Precursor of US Manipulation of World Public Opinion." Helsinki Times, November 10, 2021. https://www.helsinkitimes.fi/china-news/20343-cia-s-operation-mockingbird-a-precursor-of-usmanipulation-of-world-public-opinion.html

34. Whitney, Joel. "Exclusive: The Paris Review, the Cold War and the CIA." Salon.com, May 28, 2012. https://www.salon.com/2012/05/27/exclusive_the_paris_review_the_cold_war_and_the_cia/

35. Vulliamy, Ed. "'Rockers and Spies' – How the CIA Used Culture to Shred the Iron Curtain." The Guardian. Guardian News and Media, May 3, 2020. https://www.theguardian.com/us-news/2020/may/03/rockers-and-spies-how-the-cia-used-culture-to-shred-the-iron-curtain

36.

von Tunzelmann, Alex. "Zero Dark Thirty's Torture Scenes Are Controversial and Historically Dubious." The Guardian. Guardian News and Media, January 25, 2013. https://www.theguardian.com/film/filmblog/2013/jan/25/zero-dark-thirty-reel-history

37. Alford, Matthew. "Pentagon, CIA Deeply Involved in Hollywood Movies." PopularResistance.Org, September 10, 2017. https://popularresistance.org/pentagon-cia-deeply-involved-in-hollywood-movies/

38. "Project Monarch." Hollywood Subliminals, August 30, 2014. https://hollywoodsubliminals.wordpress.com/project-monarch/

39. Schädlich, Andreas, et al. "Accumulation of Nanocarriers in the Ovary: A Neglected Toxicity Risk?" Journal of Controlled Release. Elsevier, February 21, 2012. https://www.sciencedirect.com/science/article/abs/pii/S0168365912000892

40. Stecklow, Steve, and Andrew MacAskill. "Special Report the Ex-Pfizer Scientist Who Became an Anti-Vax Hero." Reuters. Thomson Reuters, March 18, 2021. https://www.reuters.com/investigates/special-report/health-coronavirus-vaccines-skeptic/

41. Tiffany, Kaitlyn. "A Prominent Vaccine Skeptic Returns to Twitter." The Atlantic. Atlantic Media Company, September 12, 2022. https://www.theatlantic.com/technology/archive/2022/08/alex-berenson-twitter-ban-lawsuit-covid-misinformation/671219

42. Biden, Joe. 2021. "PolitiFact - Biden Says That

Vaccinated People Can't Spread COVID-19. That's Not What CDC Says." @politifact. December 22. https://www.politifact.com/factchecks/2021/dec/22/joe-biden/biden-says-vaccinated-people-cant-spread-covid-19-/

43. Menge, Margaret. More than 11,000 people have been kicked off Twitter for sharing Covid 'misinformation'. Crossroads Report, November 27, 2022. https://crossroadsreport.substack.com/p/more-than-11000-people-have-been?utm_source=substack&utm_medium=email

44. Mason, Emily. "After PayPal Revokes Controversial Misinformation Policy, Major Concerns Remain over $2,500 Fine." Forbes. Forbes Magazine, October 29, 2022. https://www.forbes.com/sites/emilymason/2022/10/27/after-paypal-revokes-controversial-misinformation-policy-major-concerns-remain-over-2500-fine/?sh=4262fd0f30c4

45. Terr, Aaron. "Did PayPal Quietly Bring Back Its Financial Penalty for Spreading 'Misinformation'?" The Foundation for Individual Rights and Expression, October 28, 2022. https://www.thefire.org/news/did-paypal-quietly-bring-back-its-financial-penalty-spreading-misinformation

46. Leetaru, Kalev. "As Orwell's 1984 Turns 70 It Predicted Much of Today's Surveillance Society." Forbes. Forbes Magazine, August 12, 2019. https://www.forbes.com/sites/kalevleetaru/2019/05/06/as-orwells-1984-turns-70-it-predicted-much-of-todays-surveillance-society/

47. Dick, Philip K. (2002) *Selected Stories of Philip K. Dick*. New York: Pantheon ISBN 9780375421518

48. *"Snow Crash by Neal Stephenson - Penguin Books Australia"*. 2022-01-13. Archived from *the original* on 13 January 2022. Retrieved 2022-01-13.

49. "Awakening." Hollywood Subliminals, April 2, 2020. https://hollywoodsubliminals.wordpress.com/awakening/

50. Beaver, Dahria. "Predictive Programming." The Psychology of Extraordinary Beliefs, July 22, 2019. https://u.osu.edu/vanzandt/2018/04/18/predictive-programming/.

51. Neuwirth, Rostam J. "The Global Regulation of 'Fake News' in the Time of Oxymora: Facts and Fictions about the COVID-19 Pandemic as Coincidences or Predictive Programming?" International journal for the semiotics of law = Revue internationale de semiotique juridique. US National Library of Medicine, 2022. https://www.ncbi.nlm.nih.gov/pmc/articles/PMC8043095/

Chapter 10: The Global Control Matrix

1. Woodrow, Ralph. *Babylon Mystery Religion: Ancient and Modern*. Ralph Woodrow Evangelistic Association, 1981.

2. Hislop, Alexander. *The Two Babylons - Alexander Hislop*. Standard Publications, Incorporated, 2007.

3. Henning, Heath, et al. "Is Rome 'Babylon' in The Book of Revelation?" Truth Watchers, March 9, 2019. https://truthwatcher

s.com/rome-babylon-book-revelation/

4. Vigato, Marco M. *The Empires of Atlantis: The Origins of Ancient Civilizations and Mystery Traditions throughout the Ages*. Bear & Company, 2022.

5. "Home: Jesuits in Britain." Home | Jesuits In Britain. Accessed February 1, 2023. https://www.jesuit.org.uk/

6. Catholic Answers Staff. "Does 'the Black Pope' Wield the True Power in the Vatican?" Catholic Answers, September 25, 2019. https://www.catholic.com/qa/does-the-black-pope-wield -the-true-power-in-the-vatican

7. "Home: Jesuits in Britain." Home | Jesuits In Britain. Accessed February 1, 2023. https://www.jesuit.org.uk/

8. Estes, Steven. "View of Jesuit Missionary Outreach during the 19th and 20th Centuries: Global Missiology English." View of Jesuit Missionary Outreach during the 19th and 20th Centuries | Global Missiology English, July 2022. http://ojs.globalmissiolo gy.org/index.php/english/article/view/2686/6638

9. "Orsini Family." Encyclopædia Britannica. Encyclopædia Britannica, inc. Accessed February 1, 2023. https://www.britannica.co m/topic/Orsini-family

10. "The Most Powerful Man in the World? 'The Black Pope'?" Warning illuminati, September 12, 2011. https://warningilluminati.wordpress.com/the-most-pow erful-man-in-the-world-the-black-pope/

11. Sovereign Order of Malta, January 24, 2023. https://www.orde rofmalta.int/

12. "CIA Knight of Malta Vatican Connection - Internet Archive." SpirtuallySmart. Accessed January 30, 2023. https://ia800608.us.archive.org/17/items/148063172CIAKnig htsOfMaltaPdf/148063172-CIA-Knights-of-Malta-pdf.pdf

13. Arendt, James. "Famous American Members of the Knights of Malta." James Japan. December 29, 2021. https://www.jamesjpn.net/conspiracy/famous-american -members-of-the-knights-of-malta/

14. The Guardian. Undated. https://www.theguardian.com/notesa ndqueries/query/0,5753,-1551,00.html

15. Goodey, Emma. "The Order of the Garter." The Royal Family, October 17, 2022. https://www.royal.uk/order-garter

16. Good, Jonathan. "Shame and Honor: A Vulgar History of the Order of the Garter." Shame and Honor: A Vulgar History of the Order of the Garter | Reviews in History. Accessed February 2, 2023. https://reviews.history.ac.uk/review/1495

17. Trigg, Stephanie. *Shame and Honor: A Vulgar History of the Order of the Garter*. University of Pennsylvania Press, 2015. (p. 164). University of Pennsylvania Press, 2012. http://www.jstor.org/s table/j.ctt3fj4m0.

18. "Knights Templar Order - Foundations." Order of the Temple of Solomon Knights Templar Order, June 29, 2022. https://knigh

tstemplarorder.org/templar-order/templar-foundations/

19. Rule of Mystery Babylon. "The Temple Crown Owns Your Country." Arcanum Deep Secrets, August 24, 2011. https://arcanumdeepsecrets.wordpress.com/2011/08/24/the-temple-crown-owns-your-country/

20. Christmas, Matthew. "The Rose Croix." Freemasonry Matters, May 17, 2016. https://freemasonrymatters.co.uk/index.php/the-rose-croix/

21. Cain, Áine. "20 US Presidents Who Belonged to Secret Societies." Business Insider. Business Insider. Accessed February 2, 2023. https://www.businessinsider.com/us-presidents-who-were-in-secret-societies-2017-4

22. Wells H. G. 1905. *A Modern Utopia* Colonial ed. London: Fisher Unwin

23. Rivera, David Allen. "MHP: Final Warning -- the Fabians, the Round Table, and the Rhodes Scholars," 1994. https://modernhistoryproject.org/mhp?Article=FinalWarning&C=5.1

24. Rivera, David Allen. "MHP: Final Warning -- the Fabians, the Round Table, and the Rhodes Scholars," 1994. https://modernhistoryproject.org/mhp?Article=FinalWarning&C=5.1

25. Convergence, Cosmic. "Rhodes Scholars Are Not What You Thought They Were." Cosmic Convergence: 2012 and beyond. Accessed February 2, 2023. https://cosmicconvergence.org/?p=30527

26. Whitten, William. The Rhodes/Milner/Round Table Group. William's Newsletter, February 25, 2022. https://williamw.sub stack.com/p/the-rhodesmilnerround-table-group

27. "Papal Overlordship of England: The Making of an Escape Clause for Magna Carta." Medieval manuscripts blog. Accessed February 2, 2023. https://blogs.bl.uk/digitisedmanuscripts/2015/07/papal-overlor dship-of-england-the-making-of-an-escape-clause-for-magna-car ta.html#:~:text=From%20Rome%20on%2021%20April%20121 4%2C%20Pope%20Innocent,it%20looked%20like%20this%20w ould%20finally%20be%20resolved

28. Zeus, Ahuwah. "United States Corp." World Crime Syndicate. Accessed February 2, 2023. https://blacknobilityvaticancosanostra.blogspot.com/20 19/08/united-states-corp.html?view=timeslide

29. Davis, Iain. "What Is the Global Public-Private Partnership." Iain Davis, January 2, 2023. https://iaindavis.com/what-is-the-globa l-public-private-partnership/

Chapter 11: Bias Check - What If "They" Are Right?

1. Rice-Oxley, Mark, et al. "What Has the United Nations Ever Done for You? – Interactive." The Guardian. Guardian News and Media, September 15, 2015. https://www.theguardian.com/world/2015/sep/15/unit ed-nations-what-has-it-ever-done-for-you-interactive

2. Duncan. "7 Reasons Why the United Nations Is Bad for the World." Humanitarian Careers, September 19, 2022. https://humanitariancareers.com/why-united-nations-bad/#:~:t ext=The%20United%20Nations%20inability%20to%20stop%20 wars%20is,gestures%20but%20fails%20to%20follow-through%2 0with%20impactful%20actions

3. Bhaimiya, Sawdah. "Elon Musk Questioned Why Davos Is 'Even a Thing,' and Jokingly Compared the Annual Meeting of the Global Elite to Online Forum 4chan." MSN. Accessed February 2,   2023. https://www.msn.com/en-us/money/markets/elon-musk-questi oned-why-davos-is-even-a-thing-and-jokingly-compared-the-ann ual-meeting-of-the-global-elite-to-online-forum-4chan/ar-AA16 r8g6

4. Horowitz, Julia. "Davos Draws Record Crowds, but Its Relevance Is Fading | CNN Business." CNN. Cable News Network, January 16, 2023. https://www.cnn.com/2023/01/16/business /world-economic-forum-davos-deglobalization/index.html

5. Amaro, Silvia. "The Davos elite like to make bold predictions. But they don't always get them right." CNBC, January 16, 2023. https://www.cnbc.com/2023/01/13/wef-2023-the-davos -predictions-that-did-not-work-out.html

6. "Neoliberalism." Encyclopædia Britannica. Encyclopædia Britannica, inc., December 13, 2022. https://www.britannica.com/to pic/neoliberalism

7.

Buckup, Sebastian. "The End of Neoliberalism?" WEF, July 17, 2017. https://www.weforum.org/agenda/2017/07/this-is-what-the-future-of-economic-liberalism-looks-like-its-time-to-rethink-it

8. Richter, Stephan and Uwe Bott. "Klaus Schwab and the WEF Run Away from Their Past." The Globalist, October 17, 2022. https://www.theglobalist.com/world-economic-forum-klaus-schwab-neoliberalism-capitalism-corporate-responsibility/#:~:text=When%20Klaus%20Schwab%2C%20the%20founder%20of%20the%20World,increasingly%20prevailed%20in%20large%20parts%20of%20the%20world.%E2%80%9D

9. Nerger, Matt. "6 Claims Made by Climate Change Skeptics-and How to Respond." Rainforest Alliance, December 8, 2022. https://www.rainforest-alliance.org/everyday-actions/6-claims-made-by-climate-change-skeptics-and-how-to-respond/

10. van Huis, Arnold. "Edible Insects Are the Future?" The Proceedings of the Nutrition Society. US National Library of Medicine. Accessed February 2, 2023. https://pubmed.ncbi.nlm.nih.gov/26908196/

11. "Chitosan." Memorial Sloan Kettering Cancer Center. Accessed February 2, 2023. https://www.mskcc.org/cancer-care/integrative-medicine/herbs/chitosan

12. Mr, Creatonics. "Beware! These Are the 7 Most Common Types of Cryptocurrency Scams." CoinSutra, June 8, 2022. https://coinsutra.com/cryptocurrency-scams/#:~:text=Cryptoc

urrency%20scams%20that%20everyone%20should%20be%20aw
are%20of,%26%20Dump%20Groups%20...%207%207.%20Impe
rsonators%20.

13. Goswami, Rohan. "How Sam Bankman-Fried Swin-
    dled $8 Billion in Customer Money, Accord-
    ing to Federal Prosecutors." CNBC, December 19,
    2022. https://www.cnbc.com/2022/12/18/how-sam-bankman
    -fried-ran-8-billion-fraud-government-prosecutors.html

14. Delaney, Jack. "We Need a Universal Basic Income Now and after
    COVID-19." Truthout, June 7, 2020. https://truthout.org/arti
    cles/we-need-a-universal-basic-income-now-and-after-covid-19/

15. Minnicks, Margaret. "What All Religions Have in Common."
    Letterpile. Accessed February 2, 2023.
    https://letterpile.com/religion/What-All-Religions-Have-in-Co
    mmon-A-Look-at-the-Core-Beliefs-of-Worlds-Major-Faiths

16. Meek, Andy. "Cable TV Is Dying, and the Industry
    Only Has Itself to Blame." Yahoo! Accessed February 2,
    2023. https://www.yahoo.com/entertainment/cable-tv-dying-i
    ndustry-only-211216126.html

Chapter 12: The Great Resistance

1. Garland, Jess. "Democracy Made in England: Where next for
   English Local Government?" Electoral Reform Society ERS,
   March 9, 2022.
   https://www.electoral-reform.org.uk/latest-news-and-research/p

ublications/democracy-made-in-england-where-next-for-english
-local-government/

2. Smith, Sean Stein. "Bitcoin Is Showing the Power of Decentralized Money." Forbes. Forbes Magazine, March 7, 2022. https://www.forbes.com/sites/seansteinsmith/2022/03/06/bitcoin-is-showing-the-power-of-decentralized-money/?sh=68594a36af0b

3. Davies, Sam Thomas. "Book Summary: Rich Dad Poor Dad by Robert T. Kiyosaki." Sam Thomas Davies, June 21, 2022. https://www.samuelthomasdavies.com/book-summaries/business/rich-dad-poor-dad/

4. Folger, Jean. "Tax-Efficient Investing: A Beginner's Guide." Investopedia, January 24, 2023. https://www.investopedia.com/articles/stocks/11/intro-tax-efficient-investing.asp

5. Jones, Jessica. "Could Bartering Become the New Buying in a Changed World?" BBC Worklife. BBC, August 26, 2020. https://www.bbc.com/worklife/article/20200821-the-rise-of-bartering-in-a-changed-world

6. Scranton, Philip. "The Rise of the Barter Economy." Bloomberg.com. Bloomberg, September 10, 2012. https://www.bloomberg.com/opinion/articles/2012-09-10/the-rise-of-the-barter-economy?+leadSource=uverify+wall

7. Miller, Norman. "Are Community Currencies a Better Way to Shop?" BBC Worklife. BBC, April 27, 2020. https://www.bbc.com/worklife/article/20200427-how-c

ommunity-currencies-help-keep-businesses-afloat

8. Porter, Kim. "Best Peer-to-Peer Lending of January 2023." U.S. news, January 31, 2023. https://money.usnews.com/loans/personal-loans/best-peer-to-peer-lending

9. "No Evidence That Depression Is Caused by Low Serotonin Levels, Finds Comprehensive Review." ScienceDaily, July 20, 2022. https://www.sciencedaily.com/releases/2022/07/220720 080145.htm

10. Bauer, Brent A. "Herbal Treatment for Anxiety: Is It Effective?" Mayo Clinic. Mayo Foundation for Medical Education and Research, March 2, 2018. https://www.mayoclinic.org/diseases-conditions/generalized-anxiety-disorder/expert-answers/herbal-treatment-for-anxiety/faq -20057945

11. Tyrrell, Mark, and Roger Elliot. "Side Effects of Antidepressants." Clinical Depression.co.uk, October 19, 2014. https://www.clinical-depression.co.uk/dlp/treating-depression/side-effects-of-antidepressants/#:~:text=Side%20Effects%20of%2 0Antidepressants%201%20Uncovering%20the%20new,rash%2C %20and%20weight%20gain%20...%20More%20items...%20

12. "Understanding the Opioid Overdose Epidemic." Centers for Disease Control and Prevention, June 1, 2022. https://www.cd c.gov/opioids/basics/epidemic.html

13. "How Does Pranic Healing Work?" How it works – Institute of Pranic Healing UK & Ireland. Accessed February 2, 2023. https

://www.ukpranichealing.co.uk/ukpranic/how-it-works/

14. Petre, Alina. "12 Powerful Ayurvedic Herbs and Spices with Health Benefits." Healthline. Healthline Media, November 27, 2019. https://www.healthline.com/nutrition/ayurvedic-herbs#1.-Ashwagandha

15. Tencer, Daniel. "85% Of Jobs That Will Exist in 2030 Haven't Been Invented Yet: Report." HuffPost, July 14, 2017. https://www.huffpost.com/archive/ca/entry/85-of-jobs-that-will-exist-in-2030-haven-t-been-invented-yetd_ca_5cd4e7dae4b07bc72973112c

16. "What Is Unschooling?" TheSchoolRun. Accessed February 2, 2023. https://www.theschoolrun.com/what-unschooling

17. Barbieri, Annalisa. "10 Good Reasons to Home School Your Child." The Guardian. Guardian News and Media, September 10, 2016. https://www.theguardian.com/lifeandstyle/2016/sep/10/10-good-reasons-to-home-school-your-child

18. Durden, Tyler. "Get Woke, Go Broke: Disney's LGBT Kid's Film 'Strange World' Projected to Lose $147 Million." ZeroHedge. Accessed February 2, 2023. https://www.zerohedge.com/political/get-woke-go-broke-disneys-lgbt-kids-film-strange-world-projected-lose-147-million

19. Brinson, Will. "Colin Kaepernick Jersey Sales Have Skyrocketed since He Began His Protest." CBSSports.com, September 5, 2016. https://www.cbssports.com/nfl/news/colin-kaepernick-jersey-sales-have-skyrocketed-since-he-began-his-protest/

20. Jaeger, Jarryd. "Breaking: Ivan Provorov Jerseys Sell out Online after He Refuses to Wear Pride Jersey." The Post Millennial. Source: The Post Millennial, January 19, 2023. https://thepostmillennial.com/breaking-ivan-provorov-j erseys-sell-out-online-after-he-refuses-to-wear-pride-jersey

21. Cline, Austin. "Karl Marx on Religion as the Opium of the People." Learn Religions, January 7, 2019. https://www.learnreligi ons.com/karl-marx-on-religion-251019

22. Nixey, Catherine. "Britain's NHS Faces Huge Challenges in 2023." The Economist. The Economist Newspaper, November 18,   2022. https://www.economist.com/the-world-ahead/2022/11/18/brit ains-nhs-faces-huge-challenges-in-2023?utm_medium=cpc.adw ord.pd&utm_source=google&ppccampaignID=18151738051 &ppcadID=&utm_campaign=a.22brand_pmax&utm_content =conversion.direct-response.anonymous&gclid=Cj0KCQiAic6 eBhCoARIsANlox84NmVBEYnOhCjElg2gBZZDXND2SMq k_VqW1BvkAHRH6Rp-0x0AUzQAaAnl7EALw_wcB&gclsrc =aw.ds

23. McDonald, Charlotte. "How Many Earths Do We Need?" BBC News. BBC, June 15, 2015. https://www.bbc.com/news/magaz ine-33133712

Epilogue

1. Drezner, Daniel W. "The Political Economy of Document Number Nine." Foreign Policy, August 20,

2013. https://foreignpolicy.com/2013/08/20/the-political-eco nomy-of-document-number-nine/

2. Martinez, George. "FBI Says China Could Use TikTok to Spy on Americans, Including Government Workers." NPR, November 16, 2022. https://www.npr.org/2022/11/16/1137076864/fbi-says-china -could-use-tiktok-to-spy-on-americans-including-government-w orkers

3. Faria, Zachary. "Breaking: The Chinese Spyware App Is Chinese Spyware." Washington Examiner, November 17, 2022. https://www.washingtonexaminer.com/opinion/breakin g-the-chinese-spyware-app-is-chinese-spyware

4. "Top Gun: Maverick Betrays Hollywood's Weakness in China." BBC News. BBC, June 9, 2022. https://www.bbc.com/news/w orld-us-canada-61710500

5. Op India Staff. "Ex KGB Agent Yuri Bezmenov Exposes 4 Stages of Communist Takeover of a Country." OpIndia, June 19, 2020. https://www.opindia.com/2020/06/former-kgb-agent-yuri-bez menov-exposes-the-four-stages-of-a-communist-takeover-of-a-co untry-in-rare-1984-interview/

6. Jackson, Eric. "The Top 25 Most Narcissistic CEOS in Tech." Forbes. Forbes Magazine, September 19, 2013. https://www.forbes.com/sites/ericjackson/2013/09/16/t he-top-25-most-narcissistic-ceos-in-tech/?sh=3b06961868a7

7. Perkins, John. *Confessions of an Economic Hit Man.*

Berrett-Koehler, 2004.

8. Brookes, Adam. "US Plans to 'Fight the Net' Revealed." BBC News. BBC, January 27, 2006. http://news.bbc.co.uk/2/hi/am ericas/4655196.stm

9. Blackwood, Mark. "UK Government Admits Spying on British Population for Decades." World Socialist Web Site, November 14, 2015. https://www.wsws.org/en/articles/2015/11/14/spyi-n14. html

10. Harari, Yuval Noah. *Sapiens: A Brief History of Humankind*. New York: Harper, 2014. Print.

11. Harari, Yuval Noah. *Sapiens: A Brief History of Humankind*. New York: Harper, 2014. Print.

About the Author

Constantine du Bruyn served in the Armed Forces for over 20 years, deploying across the world on military operations. As he was launched from supporting conflict to conflict, he became disillusioned with government and began to question the legitimacy of the west's involvement. Instead, he decided to begin a new career in finance so he could pursue his interest in global macroeconomics and trading, only to discover he'd left one politically-controlled institution for another. As he started to realize there was a much larger, global control mechanism at play, his journey for the truth began. He left the City and travelled with his family for a few years before settling in the countryside, where he now happily homeschools his children, grows vegetables and continues his search for the truth.